THE COMPOSER AS CONTEMPORARY
General Editor: John Lade

Schubert

General editor's preface

A series of books needs a personality of its own. As its title suggests *The Composer as Contemporary* offers a distinctly individual approach to a composer and his music, whether he be a Beethoven, a Schubert, a Britten or a Janáček. Each book opens with a detailed account of the original performance of a major work, describing how it was received by its first audience and some of the influences that brought about its composition. Subsequent chapters deal with, in addition to the composer's biography, such topics as the contemporary world to which he responded, the musical forms he chose to work in, his reputation then and now. Above all it is the purpose of the books to establish the composer in the context of his lifetime and consider his music as the expression of its age.

John Lade

Other titles in the series:

Britten Christopher Headington

Schubert

PETER GAMMOND

METHUEN

Dedicated to the Shepperton music circle
and the Freewheelers

First published in Great Britain 1982
by Methuen London Ltd
11 New Fetter Lane, London EC4P 4EE

Printed in Great Britain by
Butler & Tanner Ltd, Frome and London

British Library Cataloguing in Publication data:

Gammond, Peter
Schubert.—(The Composer as contemporary)
1. Schubert—Franz 2. Composers—Austria
—Biography
I. Title II. Series
780'.92'4 ML410.S3

ISBN 0-413-46990-5

Frontispiece: watercolour of Franz Schubert by
W. A. Rieder, 1825 (*BBC Hulton Picture Library*)

The spells of the poet, the pleasures of singing,
They too will be gone, be they true as they may;
No longer will songs in our party be ringing,
For the singer too will be called away.
  The waters from source to the sea must throng.
  The singer at last will be lost in his song.

A poem by Eduard von Bauernfeld read by Schubert to his friends gathered at Schober's house on New Year's Day, 1828.

Contents

Introduction

The inscription on Schubert's grave, written by Franz Grillparzer, has become an accepted summary of his achievement: 'The art of music here entombed a rich possession but even far fairer hopes' – suggesting, by implication, that his mortal point of departure left us deprived of music that would have been finer than anything he achieved in his brief lifetime. An idle speculation at the best of times, particularly for those who believe in the pre-destined callousness of fate.

It is arguable that, in modern times, Schubert would not have died of what would now be considered quite a minor illness. Certainly the works he achieved in his last years, notably the ineffable String Quintet in C, suggest that he was on the fringes of writing his truly 'great' symphonies and chamber-music, and, who knows, he might have found his way to writing an opera that would stand beside Mozart's. It is almost impossible not to think of Mozart in connection with Schubert. Yet Mozart's early death seems not to have deprived us so cruelly, for he had already achieved true greatness so many times in so many forms.

Such speculation with regard to Schubert is irresistible; perhaps because, however highly we rate him – and that is amongst the highest ('the last of the great composers,' wrote Alfred Einstein – a statement that needs qualifying) – there is always the feeling that he had still not got his house in order; that he was an 'unfinished' composer in many ways. Robert Schumann, however, one of the first to tell the world how great Schubert was, deplored the suggestion that Schubert was fairer in hope than achievement.

The academic world of music is unduly obsessed with the idea that maturity inevitably brings depth and richness and, as a rider to this, that the more profoundly intellectual a work is, the better it is. It is by no means a provable equation. Many who have the artistic misfortune to grow old may be found to have done all the exciting things in the years of their youth. It also depends on what we mean by and find exciting. It also depends on the point at which the individual grows old. Some do it at twenty, some at forty, some as late as sixty. Some grow old and see their youthful vigour disappear; some rediscover youth in old age and become joyfully childish again. Such phenomenon as the late Beethoven quartets are always used to back the maturity argument. Perhaps Beethoven was one of those who, in spite of physical deterioration, never got really old at heart. In any case, he was only fifty-seven when he died. Mozart, dead at thirty-five, on the other hand, attained undeniable maturity with such works as the late symphonies, *The Magic Flute* and the final Requiem. Yet *The Magic Flute*, for all its profundity and wisdom, is a young work in spirit and full of moments of youthful charm. It could also be said to offer a glimpse of some of the even weightier things that Mozart might have written had he lived to be eighty; by which time, as fate may have seen, he could conceivably have written too much.

This is, indeed, all fascinatingly fruitless. Perhaps the true charm of Schubert actually lies in the fact that he was always a relatively young composer. He left the world at thirty-one, already in a surrendering frame of mind. It is unbearable to think that he might have gone into a long decline with depression and frustration at last getting the upper hand and quelling the flame of optimism that faintly persisted. Schubert died young and never wrote any oppressively mature music. It has become common to try to prove otherwise. But why should we want to? There is excitement and zest enough in what he left behind.

The fascination of Schubert lies in many paradoxes but most strongly in the fact that we can observe and point to his failings without losing any of our love and high regard for his music. If we put his output beside the other-worldliness of Bach's, the fatherly authority of Handel's, the accumulative progression of

Haydn's, the sculptured beauty of Mozart's, the powerful utterance of Beethoven's – Schubert's output can sometimes seem a bundle of rags and tatters. Yet this does not stop him from being one of the most fascinating, most lovable composers of all. It has become old-fashioned to say it, but perhaps it was his inspired amateurishness that makes him so endearing. He is the one composer who seems to be actually writing and exploring in front of us. If we can often see why he went wrong we are even more excited when he goes right. For then his music suddenly seems, as perhaps music ought more often, to be essentially magic. If Schubert, in solid analysable terms, was not the greatest of all composers, he was, surely, the great magician of them all in turning those black dots on five undeviating lines into a moving expression of the human spirit.

The 'Unfinished' Symphony of 1822 was some years away in time from his maturity, yet it is widely seen as one of his deepest journeys into the world of the unknown. So profound, in its utterance, they say, that Schubert simply gave up trying to finish it and ended in mid-bar. Did he run out of that elusive elixir called inspiration, or did he perhaps run out of youthfulness at that point? It has remained one of the great mysteries of music; yet, like the armless masterpieces of Greek statuary, we could hardly hope for it to be any better if the missing bits were restored. It is an unfinished symbol of an unfinished life – and that is where we might well begin.

I 'Unfinished' Symphony

Schubert wrote a symphony – Too bad he didn't finish it!
from a popular song of the 1930s

In the autumn of 1822, in a Europe trying to regain some composure after the predatory ravages of Napoleon, but heading for an even more painful pageant of human disasters, Franz Schubert was a twenty-five-year-old freelance composer, probably instinctively aware of his potential and sure of his mission in life, but somewhat disheartened by the meagre results of his dedicated labours. Beyond the narrow limits of a part of Viennese society and a little of Austria nearby he was virtually unknown, though, to balance this to some extent, he was deeply loved and admired by a discerning circle of friends and intellectual compatriots. Pure ability, even amounting to genius, tends to come to nothing in the world if not helped either by good fortune or the irresistible self-confidence of the idiot. Schubert's reticent and private personality had much to do with his commercial neglect. He could have cultivated the friendship of the rich and powerful, but it was never a part of his nature to do so. He lived for many years within calling distance of the man he most admired, Ludwig van Beethoven, but he never summoned up the courage to force a close acquaintanceship. The great man was probably hardly aware of his rival-to-be in the textbooks of the future. But when not afflicted by the regular doubts and depressions that assail the creative artist, Schubert was certain enough of his destiny to be totally absorbed in music-making during his days; recharging himself with the delights of wine and companionship in the evenings.

By this time he was, in fact, first realising himself as a published composer. His first songs had been printed in the spring of 1821 and from then on he enjoyed regular, if sparse, publication. April 1822 had seen the issue of his *Eight Variations on a French Song* and his eighth book of *Lieder*, and each month had seen some public or private performance of one of his works – mostly quartets and other small-scale efforts rather than the bigger things that he would have liked to have seen appreciated; but at least he now enjoyed some reasonable, if limited, acclaim. To balance the assets, he was already a continual martyr to ill-health and was suffering acutely from the physical and mental agony of the syphilis he had contracted through succumbing to the persuasions of his riotous friend Schober, with whom he was living in 1822. All such considerations have their importance as we try to decide upon the frame of mind in which Schubert embarked upon one of his potentially greatest works which later, very much later, was to become known as the 'Unfinished' Symphony.

The facts and theories surrounding this musical mystery are, in the end, completely baffling. No amount of supposition, however reasoned, can completely persuade us of the truth of the matter. Only the discovery of the rest of the work (which must now be assumed highly unlikely) can ever settle the argument. A mere state of incompletion can prove nothing. If we are to believe Schubert's own dating of manuscripts, which was generally accurate and helpful (though not always), he began work on the B minor Symphony on 30 October 1822. At this time, greatly influenced by Beethoven whose symphonies were the great popular works of contemporary Vienna, he plunged into the one work that, of all his compositions, might be said to show the strongest influence of the revered master; influence by way of example, rather than method. Earlier in the year Schubert had completed his most substantial opera, *Alfonso and Estrella*, and his Mass in A flat. The former was promised a production by Weber but Schubert spoilt his chances there by speaking slightingly of the composer's *Euryanthe*. He was never able to persuade anyone else to produce it, and it was not performed until 1882.

Judging from the results, in a strangely inspired mood and in emotional turbulence, but presumably in no great state of expectancy as to its outcome, Schubert worked on a piano sketch of the new symphony. He quickly produced the first two movements and, so far as is known, only the outline of a third movement, a scherzo. By 30 October he had started to score the work and sometime in November it is believed that the orchestral score of the first two movements was completed. In November he wrote the *Wanderer* Fantasia and in December a handful of songs including *Der Musensohn*. At this point the mystery begins, for we have no further definite clue from Schubert himself or from others as to whether he continued to work on the symphony or whether he simply discarded it. By his own standards of productivity he would have been comparatively idle during these months if he was, in fact, not working on the symphony.

At the beginning of 1823 he was still unwell and unable to leave the house. He turned down a request for a vocal quartet as he considered he had lately indulged in that form too much. An undated letter, placed by Deutsch at the beginning of 1823, states that he had 'nothing for full orchestra which I could send out into the world with a clear conscience' which, in view of later happenings, does not suggest a composer who would happily send out an incompleted work – a work which would have been lying on his desk at the time. In February the *Wanderer* Fantasia was published and he sent *Alfonso and Estrella* to Ignaz Mosel, a director of the Court Theatre, for his opinion. On 10 April 1823, the Styrian Musical Society in Graz had considered a proposition that 'Herr Franz Schubert of Vienna be admitted a non-resident honorary member, the said composer, although still young, having already proved by his compositions that he will one day take a high rank as tone-poet and be sure to show gratitude to the Styrian Musical Society for having first made him an honorary member of a not unimportant association.' In the middle of April they wrote to Schubert:

> The services you have so far rendered to the art of music are too well known for the Committee of the Styrian Musical

> Society to have remained unaware of them. The latter, being desirous of offering you proof of their esteem, have elected you as a non-resident honorary member of the Styrian Musical Society. A Diploma to that effect as well as a copy of the Society's Statutes is enclosed herewith.

A similar diploma had been sent to Beethoven in January 1822, with the slight difference that Schubert was referred to as having 'already generally acknowledged merits' whereas Beethoven was referred to as 'the greatest composer of this present century'.

The diploma was delivered to Schubert through Anselm Hüttenbrenner of Graz via his brother Josef who lived in Vienna. He did not receive the diploma until September, as he had been away from Vienna trying to get rid of his infection (and in the meantime had been given a diploma by the Linz Musical Society), and wrote his letter of thanks on 20 September 1823:

> I am greatly obliged by the diploma of honorary membership you so kindly sent me, and which, owing to my prolonged absence from Vienna, I received only a few days ago. May it be the reward of my devotion to the art of music to become wholly worthy of such a distinction one day. In order to give musical expression to my sincere gratitude as well I shall take the liberty before long of presenting your honourable Society with one of my Symphonies in full score.

The chronology so far dispels the frequent suggestion that Schubert originally wrote his symphony *for* the Graz Styrian Society.

The first question that arises at this point is whether Schubert, during the course of almost a whole year, some of it spent at the Kremsmunster Monastery (which has presumably been well searched in the ensuing years), and in spite of his affliction, never felt the urge or inspiration necessary to complete the score of the B minor Symphony. There is also the added complication of an E major symphony, started in 1821 and left in an even greater state of incompletion (which rather throws the argument in the opposite direction). Some commentators (including that most assiduous Schubert documentor, Otto Erich Deutsch, to whom we owe the definitive Schubert catalogue*) feel compelled to remark that they find it incredible that Schubert should think of sending the Styrian Society just two movements of a symphony with one sheet of the scherzo. He could hardly have expected it to be performed in this state! He was far from being famous enough to expect his fragments to be considered holy relics, and was already in contention with the usual conservatism of the establishment. But then neither, perhaps, did he see it himself as the acknowledged masterpiece that it was to become: one of the most often played and most revered works of the late nineteenth and twentieth centuries. There is a possibility that Schubert thought nothing of it at all, as he seems to have made no mention of the work again during his lifetime, despite his continued association with the Hüttenbrenner brothers. Schubert, as we know, was very much in the habit of leaving works incomplete or in the shape of isolated movements, so our emotional arguments to the contrary are tellingly counterbalanced in this respect. Even Schubert's brother Ferdinand, with whom he was very close, and who catalogued his works after his death, was totally unaware of the existence of the B minor Symphony.

It is only from later vague memories and subsequent documentation that the history of the manuscript is pieced together; but with no explanations ever given as to what actually happened or why. Soon after writing his letter to the Styrian Society in September 1823, Schubert is said to have handed over the incomplete (or complete?) symphony to Josef Hüttenbrenner, in the street on his way to the General Hospital, so that he could pass it on to his brother Anselm in Graz, who could then hand it over to the Styrians. The whole episode now becomes a total mystery with no enlightenment being given by any of the participants. A brief explanation of the Hüttenbrenners' involvement

* Please see the Appendix for information about Deutsch catalogue numbers which have been used to date Schubert's works in this book and appear thus: (D331).

must be made here, though they will be more fully dealt with later. Anselm and Josef had been fellow students with Schubert under Salieri and remained his closest friends till his death; a fact which in no way helps us elucidate the mystery. Josef was a great admirer of Schubert and was continually making attempts to promote his music. It is doubly strange, therefore, that he should have done nothing about this work in the ensuing years.

It is authoritatively stated in some sources that Josef himself kept the manuscript for four years until 1827 before handing it over to his brother Anselm. Why should he do this? Did he, perhaps, advise Schubert that an incomplete symphony was not an acceptable offering to the Society, and held it back hoping for the rest to materialise? It is not until 1850 that he spoke about it to Kreissle von Hellborn, Schubert's first biographer, who was then preparing the volume that was finally published in 1865. Kreissle makes the statement:

> Of the more important works composed in this year [1822] we may cite: An orchestral symphony in B minor, which Schubert presented, in a half-finished state, to the Musikverein at Gratz, in return for the compliment paid to him of being elected an honorary member of that society. Josef Hüttenbrenner is my authority for saying that the first and second movements are entirely finished and the third (Scherzo) partly. The fragment in the possession of Herr Anselm Hüttenbrenner, of Gratz, is said, the first movement particularly, to be of great beauty.

By 1860 Josef Hüttenbrenner was giving a slightly different version of the circumstances to Johann Herbeck, at that time conductor of the Musikfreunde Society in Vienna and the symphony's first promoter, telling him: 'My brother [Anselm] possesses a treasure in Schubert's B minor Symphony which we place on a level with any of Beethoven's. But it isn't finished, Schubert gave it to me for Anselm as thanks for having sent him, through me, the Diploma of Honour of the Graz Music Society.'

At least there is some consistency as to the state of incompleteness of the symphony.

Whether Josef kept it for four years, or immediately handed it over to his brother, as other historians say, is immaterial only in the absence of a general explanation of this mystery. Knowledge of what passed between him and Schubert would be very significant. Anyway, the manuscript, sooner or later, came into the possession of Anselm, who is generally painted as the real villain of the piece, a scheming, tenth-rate composer, only thinking of his own interests (aided and abetted by his brother Josef who switched his promotional efforts to him after Schubert's death), who suppressed Schubert's work for his own ends. It is hard to imagine what those ends could really have been. The performance of a superb symphony by Schubert, at his instigation, could hardly have hindered his own chances. Whatever the thinking of these two, who are on record elsewhere as actively trying to promote some of Schubert's works (his operas, for example), the second astonishing fact seems to be beyond doubting: namely, that Anselm had the work in his possession until 1865 and said nothing further about it. Even Schubert's brother remained unaware of its existence; and most inexplicably of all (unless we accept some later theories about his own actions) Schubert himself chose to make no further mention of the work. Here, of course, we are inclined to speculate to the limits of frustration. Were the Hüttenbrenners really villains? Did they keep as their own dark secret a work that was intended for the Music Society, or did they consider it a personal gift of friendship? Did they try to persuade Schubert to finish the work, without avail? Did they perhaps not have the acumen to consider it a great work until the world in general had affirmed its acceptance of Schubert's genius? One wonders if the Styrian Society themselves ever made any enquiries, as Schubert's reputation grew, about the symphony they had been promised.

But, again, most baffling of all is Schubert's own acquiescent silence. Surely he must have wondered what had happened to it, unless we accept the widely-held opinion that he never felt able to progress beyond those first two supreme movements and remained unable to match them. The piano sketches for the scherzo might reasonably be considered not to have lived up to the rest (a matter of varied opinion), but during the six years that followed he would surely have found time and inspiration to write something better. There is one curious hint in a letter that he wrote in March 1824, in which he describes his later quartets and the octet as 'paving the way for [another*] grand symphony'. We are left open to speculation as to whether he thought that he had already written a 'grand' symphony. None of the others, apart from the 'Unfinished', can really be considered 'grand'. The assumption now is that it was the 'Great' C major Symphony which was, in fact, the one written at Gastein and previously presumed missing.

Leaving these realms of speculation, with Schubert's manuscript gathering dust in a chest or drawer in Anselm's lumber-room or even, melodramatically, being used as material to start the fire by his servants (as, apparently, happened to some other Schubert manuscripts in his possession, including some of the operas), we can return to the semifactual story. In 1865, Johann Herbeck (who waited yet another five years before acting on Josef's information) went (on the authority of Johann's son Ludwig) to visit the ageing, 'crafty-eyed' and still unsuccessful Anselm at Ober-Andritz, near Graz, and persuaded him to produce the Schubert manuscript. Even then, it was apparently difficult to persuade the old man that the treasure belonged to the world and not to him alone. But he saw it as a good bargaining point and, only after Herbeck had promised to perform some of his own orchestral works in Vienna, at the same time as the Schubert symphony, did he bring forth the score: two completed movements and one sheet, which gives the impression of a clear intention to continue, with the fragment of the scherzo. This was, of course, how the manuscript had long been described, so Herbeck had no reason to suspect that Anselm might have

* The word 'another' is omitted from some translations; its addition or omission certainly gives the whole statement a different weight.

separated the rest of the symphony either then or previously. If, in fact, he had discovered his housemaids using the rest of it for kindling paper on some earlier occasion he would hardly have cared to admit to such carelessness. Speculation can only get wilder at this point: and the case is generally left to rest on the assumption that Schubert was not interested in completion, or was not able to match the first two movements (which, to most people, still seems nonsense in the light of what he later produced). Or, of course, that there was a complete symphony which was either partly suppressed or suffered some less dignified mishap. Did Anselm keep the rest and destroy the pages before he died in 1868? He remained artistic director of the Styrian Music Society until 1839 without ever revealing his secret and he had carefully burnt his own diaries in 1841. In 1853 he had produced a piano duet version of Schubert's symphony which was never published. Josef Hüttenbrenner died in 1881, still proclaiming himself the 'prophet, singer, friend and pupil' of Schubert, and still keeping firmly to the 'legend' of the 'Unfinished' Symphony.

Johann Herbeck took the manuscript back to Vienna and had it copied ready for a memorable first performance at the Musikvereinsaal on 17 December 1865, just over forty-three years after Schubert had first conceived it. Still feeling that 'unfinished' symphonies were not quite respectable, he added the finale of the D major Symphony (No. 3). For the next performance in 1866, it was assumed that such an addition was no longer necessary. An audience of distinguished musicians, who had travelled from all over the world for this great event, added to the packed and expectant house. Imagine hearing that soft unison opening for cello and basses for the first time! Then, at bar 42, the simple, unforgettable melody that the cellos introduce! At this point the audience could not restrain their delight; and there was such tumultuous applause at the end that the whole work was repeated.

Present at that famous first night was the critic Eduard Hanslick. After a firm condemnation of Anselm's contempt for posterity and a quick dismissal of his own music, there followed a description of the 'Schubert novelty'. Hanslick wrote:

> When, after the few introductory bars, clarinet and oboe in unison began their gentle cantilena above the calm murmur of the violins, every child recognised the composer and a muffled 'Schubert' was whispered in the audience. He had hardly entered, but it seemed that one recognised him by his step, by way of opening the door. And when, after this nostalgic cantilena in the minor, there followed the contrasting G major theme of the violoncellos, a charming song of almost *Ländler*-like intimacy, every heart rejoiced, as if, after a long separation, the composer himself were among us in person.

Hüttenbrenner's music was completely ignored and, in fact, neither of the brothers even attended the concert.

So, whatever doubts Schubert himself may have had about the work, if any, they were well and truly contradicted within moments of the first bars being heard for the first time. Thereafter, the 'Unfinished' Symphony never looked back and remained firmly in the popular repertoire. It was published in December 1866 by Spina in Vienna. The first London performance was given at the Crystal Palace on 6 April 1867. With these two tantalising movements now in the world's possession, a ceaseless barrage of theory and speculation ranged around the work. August Ludwig became the first person to supply it with two supplementary movements. In 1928, the centenary of Schubert's death was celebrated with a competition, organised by the Columbia Graphophone Company, offering a prize for the best completion of the symphony. One of the winners was Frank Merrick who managed to produce a good Schubert pastiche.

There was obviously a limited future in providing extra movements that were not written by Schubert, and most effort was put into trying to solve the problem of the missing part and to surmising on the nature of Schubert's intentions. There was no doubt about the intended scherzo, for the piano sketch existed as well as the orchestral fragment. A small but not conclusive point, noted in Grove and elsewhere, is that the final page of the full orchestral score of the scherzo has notes tied over to the next missing page – a curious way to end the venture, and a strong suggestion that Schubert either did, or intended to, continue. Since the reappearance of the 'Unfinished' several people have provided an orchestrated reconstruction of the scherzo, notably Gerald Abraham, who produced a convincing score, using the melody of Schubert's song *Der Leidende* for the trio, which was a convincing substitute for the sort of thing that the composer might have provided. But what if the final movement could in fact be found amongst Schubert's subsequent works, having been used, as composers so often did in those days, for another purpose? The first hint was found in an 1888 Crystal Palace performance which added the B minor entr'acte from *Rosamunde* as a substitute movement. Einstein, in his 1951 book on Schubert, also dropped hints in this direction, describing the entr'acte as 'the symphonic link between the 'Unfinished' and the C major Symphony'.

The *Rosamunde* music was being composed in the autumn of 1823 at about the time when Schubert was due to hand over the symphony to the Hüttenbrenners. Hard-pressed to complete the task, it has been suggested that he might simply have removed the final movement from the symphony and added it to the incidental music for the play. There are other coincidental pointers: the fact that the music was in B minor to start with; that it was scored for identical instruments; and that he did make use of various other snippets of his music – the A minor Quartet for one, the song *Der Leidende* for another. So it is at the least a tenable proposition which works quite well in performance. The theory had a firm supporter in Arthur Hutchings, in his volume on Schubert in the *Master Musicians* series, who said:

> Incontrovertible seems Professor Gerald Abraham's evidence that the B minor entr'acte, stylistically incongruous with *Rosamunde*, was intended as the finale of this symphony, of which

> it is worthy. Even more difficult to deny is the musical evidence of one's ears when this piece concludes the work.

He goes further to declare that 'we should no longer present this work as a torso'.

But, however well Abraham's re-creation falls on the ears, and adopting the assumption that Schubert would have ended the work in B minor after the E major of the slow movement and the intended scherzo in B minor, the completion must be accepted with reservation simply because we do not know that it is what he intended. Two more pages of the orchestrated scherzo came to light in 1969 which neither repudiated nor confirmed Schubert's intentions. In fact, in a world where too much music tends to go on for too long, well beyond the listener's satiation point, if not the composer's or the academician's, we are happy to have the 'Unfinished' Symphony as it is, with its two well-balanced and not dissimilar movements still offering, emotionally and musically, a consummate experience. Growing naturally from the world of Schubert's unsurpassed *Lieder*, it may not have achieved Schubert's aim of producing a completed 'great' symphony; a mantle and name which the more diffuse and conservative Symphony in C was to take on with justification. Had the B minor Symphony been heard in 1823 it might have seemed a difficult and over-ambitious work. By 1865, Wagner was well in his stride and *Tristan* was in existence. In this light the 'Unfinished' was heard in a natural context and as a delightful return to the unassuming world of song that Schubert had so effectively adorned with so little reward in his lifetime.

If the C major Symphony now seems a logical culmination of his symphonic efforts, the 'Unfinished', like some of his later quartets, was a remarkable sortie toward the romantic heights that he would have surely scaled had he lived longer. It is Schubert at his most profound and in the world of the C major Quintet. It is typical of him on several levels: melodically sublime, emotionally disturbing, and, even in the very fact of it being 'unfinished', it is a meaningful symbol of his career as a composer, his inhibitions as a person; the encapsulation of a life and creativity that ended sadly and certainly remained 'unfinished'.

II Background

1 HISTORY AND POLITICS

The German Emperor Franz II of Hapsburg-Lorraine succeeded to the Austrian throne in 1792 to be immediately thrust into a bitter war with the revolutionary forces of France. The struggle, with all the turbulence and unrest that it caused, was to continue until the important Congress of Vienna in 1814. Thereafter Viennese life assumed a superficial appearance of settled, middle-class-dominated conservative life; its respectable calm, however, only achieved by oppressive policing and the activities of informers that forced Austrian intellectual life into a private sort of culture that fostered what is now labelled the Biedermeier*

* The adjective Biedermeier, in connection with the Vienna of Schubert's time, is used constantly yet without precise definition. Perhaps in the end such a definition is impossible, just as it is for such similarly used terms as Regency or Victorian. They give us an idea of period (the Biedermeier period generally being taken as roughly 1815–50) but the evocations and styles they evoke really only apply to a very small segment of society – namely the well-to-do middle- and upper-middle classes that could afford to pursue fashion for its own sake and who, for social and financial reasons, became the supporting customers of art. The original Biedermeier was a character in a comic journal *Fliegende Blätter* and was an unsophisticated, conservative philistine who wrote bland verses that became known as *Biedermeierlieder*. He became, from a rather cynical viewpoint, the epitome and symbol of the cosy, fashionable drawing-room society that carried on its elegant and intellectual life in graceful private homes away from the prying eyes of the state police and in contrived ignorance of all the political upheaval and bloody strife that was tearing the ordinary world apart. Schubert's admirers try to diminish the point that he was, at least musically speaking, one of the corner-stones of this society, providing cosy songs whose subjects are literary, philosophical and amatory rather than involved in the sordidness of political and social considerations. So, as with the term Victorian, Biedermeier implies a drawing-room culture. Art was Biedermeier if it was elegant and refined; ceased to be so when it was in any way cosmopolitan, popular or controversial. It was the art of romantic escapism.

period. So Schubert's life (1797–1828) had a continuous background of political and intellectual upheaval and covered a vital period of Austrian history, dominated by important artistic figures. While there is no doubt that he was acutely aware of this background, and was intimately acquainted with many of its leading lights and held beliefs strong enough to occasionally add his own utterances to the general clamour, his nature mainly led him to withdraw into a private musical world and an unobtrusive existence in drawing-rooms and coffeehouses. Indeed, it was probably the disturbed quality of life at the time and the overwhelming rivalry of so many dominating personalities that were partly responsible for the submergence of his creations both from a personal and public aspect.

Prior to the succession of Franz II, Vienna had gone through a fruitful period of rebuilding in the typical baroque style of the city. Its cultural life was flourishing with a plethora of theatres and opera-houses; music was particularly alive, with such figures as Haydn, Mozart and Beethoven in full spate. Franz II's succession was backed by a justified wave of optimism. The clouds, however, had already begun to gather over distant Paris where, in 1793, Louis XVI and Marie Antoinette (the aunt of Franz II) had been executed in the cause of the French Revolution. The crowned heads of Europe could hardly regard their own positions as sacrosanct and the family web of Hapsburgs tried to wage an establishment coalition war against the revolutionary forces from 1792 onwards. Revolutionary sympathisers within Austria were savagely and to some extent needlessly suppressed, culminating in the Jacobite trials of 1794, when harsh sentences were passed on many whose guilt was scarcely proven. It was simply an intimidating warning which Austrian revolutionaries had to accept. The retribution was to come from elsewhere.

In the spring of 1796 Austrian forces were attacked on the Rhine and, in the beginning of 1797, attempting to save Mantua on their Italian border, were defeated at Arcola and Rivoli. The French armies, led by the young Napoleon Bonaparte, took control of Lombardy and Upper Italy, and started to advance through Styria and Carinthia with obvious intent to march on Vienna. Vienna was only lightly prepared, with an inefficient army bolstered by the calling-up of a volunteer corps in the autumn of 1796, one division of which went off to support the Italian Army, without success. Beethoven wrote a 'Song of Farewell to the Citizens of Vienna' and Haydn was commissioned to write a 'People's Hymn' which was sung in the Viennese theatres in February 1797, neither of which did much to stave off the impending disasters. In the midst of all this Schubert was born in an impoverished kitchen in the suburb of Liechtental.

Soon after his capture of Mantua, Napoleon crossed the Alps and occupied Graz, the main city of Styria. In Vienna panic and despair were widespread. The well-to-do got out of the city as quickly as they could and made for their country retreats; the inhabitants of outlying villages and towns hastened to Vienna to take refuge behind its ancient and inadequate fortifications, thus causing confusion on the roads, and finding a serious shortage of food and accommodation in the city. In April 1797 there was a general mobilisation of all troops and available manpower. The troops set out singing a new 'War Song of the Austrians' contributed by Beethoven, which no doubt stirred the young Schubert in his cot, as they marched down the Nussdorferstrasse to take up defensive positions in the outlying rural districts of Vienna and along the Danube. For the moment the comic-opera show of forces achieved its purpose. Napoleon, taking calm stock of the position, considered that his scattered forces might well get their lines of communication cut and on 18 April, only one day after Austria had sworn in her new 'volunteer' army, he signed the preliminary Treaty of Leoben with the Austrian government and returned to North Italy in possession of the provinces of Lombardy and Flanders, leaving Venetia to the Austrians.

A certain sense of triumph and optimism once more prevailed for some time and further threats by Napoleon's army in 1800 were not taken quite so seriously, in spite of French victories at

Marengo and Hohenlinden. Minor skirmishes won by the Austrian armies under Archduke Karl led to a triumphant welcome back to Vienna in December 1800 and a feeling that they had won the war. Austria was even able to make some token demonstration of future independence. In response to Napoleon declaring himself Emperor of France in 1804, Franz II graciously accepted the title of Emperor of Austria and had himself crowned as Franz I of Austria in August. He was to resign as Emperor of Germany in 1806, thus nominally freeing Austria of long German domination. Napoleon's actual crowning took place in December and a few days later the proclamation of the Imperial Charter of Austria was made from the balcony of the Am Hof Church. Not that it excited the population of Vienna very much, for they had always assumed their right to such a status.

The cold war continued, however, and the Hapsburgs optimistically and purposefully continued their coalition defiance of Napoleon. They attacked the French Army at Ulm and suffered an ignominious defeat. A few days later they achieved a minor victory in Italy but this time they had gone too far. Napoleon, now greatly strengthened in ambition and military power, simply marched into Vienna, meeting virtually no resistance, and occupied the city on 13 November 1805. He took up residence in Schönbrunn Palace and in December issued a conciliatory proclamation, putting the citizens on their trust as new members of the French Empire, handed power back to the Austrian authorities and moved all his troops out by 12 January 1806. It had been the first time that French troops had entered Vienna since 1683 and it left the Viennese in a somewhat unsettled state.

Emperor Franz now deemed a peaceful coexistence with the French the best course and did his best to play down the implications of the Hapsburg coalitions. Anti-French feeling, however, gained strength and by 1809 the Austrian armies had reformed and Austria decided that it would attempt, singlehanded, to free Europe of the French domination. The moment seemed opportune for Napoleon, by then, was deeply involved in suppressing the Spaniards. He soon settled this matter and inflicted several defeats on the Austrian armies that caused some misgivings in Vienna, particularly as little had been done to improve the city's fortifications. Franz I made the gesture of ordering Vienna's defence but the French Army simply marched in, installing Napoleon once again at Schönbrunn. On 1 May 1809 French artillery opened fire on the city. The ragged volunteer forces held out for a while but on 13 May the French Army again marched through the streets, now deserted and unwelcoming. The sullen resistance was stronger than before and there were many serious clashes between citizens and occupying soldiers, especially when occasional Austrian victories elsewhere caused temporary moments of optimistic patriotism. There were several months of unrest and bloodshed. The troops remained in the city until November while the swings and roundabouts of war produced defeats for Napoleon at Aspern, but a great victory at Wagram which led to a further peace treaty with Austria signed in Vienna and depriving Austria of still more territory. When the French soldiers departed on 20 November they took the precaution of blowing up all the city's fortifications which did not please the Viennese at all.

Peace reigned again, of a sort, with Austria smouldering under the French domination and angry at her loss of territory. In 1811 the country, impoverished by these long years of war, went bankrupt. The economy of Vienna was in ruins, prices soared astronomically, and resentment became white-hot. In 1812, Franz, along with the King of Prussia, was forced to pay homage to Napoleon, then departing on his disastrous Russian campaign. The following year Frederick William III managed to rouse the Hapsburg forces to proper battle pitch and united Austria, Prussia and Russia in a concerted war of liberation against France. Cheering news came with a great victory against the depleted Napoleonic forces at Leipzig in 1813, followed by the entry of the allied armies into Paris in March 1814. Vienna, even before the battles had finished, began to prepare for a new era and, in September 1814, the famous Congress of Vienna began, uniting all the European heads of state and diplomats in a gathering whose prime purpose of reshaping the continent and eradicating memories of Napoleon provided off-duty occasions for balls, banquets and country outings. It led the Prince de Ligne to make his famous remark 'Congress dances'. But it was also seen in its true light, even by those as involved as Archduke Johann, who saw it all as a round of 'miserable bartering', as an unsteady foundation of European peace. How could something based almost entirely upon acquisition, greed, retribution and national pride be anything else? Like all such international festivals it made some quick money for the trades-people; but such lavish high-living hardly endeared itself to the revolutionary element who still waited their time. Austria got back all her old possessions except Flanders and the Rhine provinces, resuming the boundaries more or less of the old Austro-Hungarian Empire, gaining Venetia and the northern territories of Italy that included Milan: a total area of some 250,000 square miles and a 30,000,000 population that was an uneasy mixture of Germans, Italians, Slavs and genuine Austrians, some 27,000,000 of whom were Roman Catholics. On the debit side Austria had lost nearly a million men in the struggles with Napoleon, which were not yet over. The last act of the Vienna Congress was signed on 9 June 1815 but already in March Napoleon had escaped from his exile on Elba and made a triumphant return to Paris to begin the famous 'hundred days'. Vienna was not able to rest easy until his final defeat at Waterloo on 18 June.

The rest of the years until Schubert's death in 1828 were reasonably settled. The revolutionary elements were too weakened to offer any great threat and their day of revolution was going to have to be delayed until 1848. The intellectual Biedermeier society simply avoided clashes with the still heavily police-backed authorities, and literary, artistic and musical life was resumed in the drawing-rooms and coffee-houses.

2 MUSIC AND LITERATURE

Through all this political upheaval life in Vienna had tottered on under the benignly ineffectual non-guidance of its restricted mayors and councils. Schubert came into a musical world dominated by the steadying influence of Haydn and the disturbing lead of the forward-looking Beethoven; while the academic side went on its quiet conservative way under the guidance of such as Salieri. As Schubert reached maturity around 1820 and began to see some of his work published, he was living in a world ruled by the powerful figures of Chancellor Metternich and Police Chief Sedlnitzky. But even their suppressive rule could do little to submerge the naturally ebullient artistic life of Vienna. So many artists, writers and musicians, actors and intellectuals gravitated toward this natural European cultural hub on the Danube, the most blatantly civilised of all cities, with its grand baroque architecture, innumerable galleries, theatres and concert-halls, its spacious gardens and elegant palaces, that actual suppression was beyond the powers of the police and politicians. Vienna turned all creative artists and all creative arts into manifestations of the romantic spirit. The works of Haydn and Mozart, although generally labelled 'classical', took on warmth and humanity and became the beginnings of modern music through the newly romantic feeling they acquired in the Viennese aura. Beethoven continued in the trend, and Schubert, in his own quiet way, the one genuine Viennese-born composer among them, established the true romantic spirit in music, at least in his most important contribution, his songs. He admired and supported the heroic spirit of such as Karl Theodor Körner (who was killed in action against the French in 1813) and the greatest national writer that Vienna produced, Franz Grillparzer. Although his essential theme was the glory of Austria, accompanied by a wholesale support for the Hapsburg tradition, the authorities were so bemused by his basic scepticism that they subjected him to a curiously contorted kind of censorship. Schiller had suffered in the same way. Vienna was alive with such activities that kept, so it is estimated in 1812, some eighty-four theatres in business. Grillparzer's protégé, Eduard von Bauernfeld, a successful writer of comedies, was one of Schubert's circle of friends. The majority of his friends belonged, in fact, to the artistic and literary world rather than the musical. The bond was simply the growing romantic era, a delight in nature and a growing interest in human rights. The most obvious influence on Schubert was a literary one, revealed in the texts and librettos that he chose to set in his vocal and theatrical music.

The musical influences on Schubert, those that helped to formulate his own style by offering paths down which he might wander before finding his own true colours, are really more difficult to ascertain. Schubert tended to keep away from other musicians and composers – perhaps simply through natural shyness and modesty. Those amongst his close acquaintances were of the lesser breed. Yet Schubert, unlike Mozart, was rarely contemptuous of those he might, with justification, have felt of inferior mettle to his own. He genuinely admired anyone who managed to write music professionally and have it published. Mostly, we can only guess at the music with which he came into contact by virtue of its being available in published form or in performances of the time.

Of the musicians of the past he was most clearly influenced by Mozart. It would have been difficult to be otherwise. It was an era of Mozart worship, with *The Magic Flute* established as Vienna's favourite opera, even if this was by virtue of its story as much as its music. It was Mozart Schubert thought of in private and mentioned most in his limited writings. Mozart was his divine example and, when he attempted to write his early symphonies, it was the spirit of Mozart that haunted them, the style of Mozart that helped him formulate his own, the music of Mozart that he most blatantly copied in his experimental days, with many traceable references in his own writings. Mozart died in 1791, six years before Schubert was born, and was strongly coming into his own, in compensation for neglect in Austria shown in his lifetime. By 1812 it is believed that Schubert had heard *The Magic Flute* and it had set his own operatic ambitions alight. In his school days he was in contact with people who had known and worked with Mozart, such as the director of the school, Dr Wilhelm Bauer, who had met him as a boy. As early as 1816 Schubert had written in his diary about the immortal Mozart whose G minor Quintet he had heard at a concert in June. And, of course, his teacher Salieri had been a great rival of Mozart and must often have talked to Schubert about him. Mozart's son, of the same Christian names, was a pianist and composer who was in Vienna until around 1820 when he heard Schubert's opera *Die Zwillingsbrüder* (*The Twin Brothers*). The critics, somewhat unkindly, compared Schubert's attempts at writing a comic opera with Mozart's achievements in this field. Schubert knew the works of this master extensively and was not afraid to allow their greatness to guide him.

No other predecessor seems to have had quite the same impact. We know that he studied Bach's fugues, and no doubt some of Bach's church music was at the back of his mind when he composed his fairly formal and unadventurous masses. But it is probably generally true to say that Bach and his great German contemporary, Handel, although their works were regularly performed in Vienna, had little to offer a questing young romanticist. Some debt to Clementi, whose works were undoubtedly amongst his possessions and which he no doubt played, as any young pianist would, is discernible in his piano music.

The figures that influenced him more, quite expectedly, were the living musicians who worked and played around him, with a success that he envied. Haydn hardly counted as he died in 1809 when Schubert was only twelve. He followed in the master's footsteps to the extent of having connections with the Esterházy family, and had a deep reverence for him, but his music (which has really only fully come into its right acceptance in very recent times) may have seemed of a much older generation to Schubert. Haydn's operas were as neglected as his own and mainly enjoyed only private performances at Esterház.

After Mozart, the greatest influence on Schubert's musical

life was Beethoven, although it was an influence that Schubert always seems to have realised to be dangerous if he was ever to find his own identity. But Beethoven was the great master of his day, admired from afar as a person, performed everywhere with due respect and heard by the apprentice Schubert, who attended Beethoven concerts and performances as often as he could afford. From Fritz Hartmann's diary, 29 March 1827: 'I went to the Castle of Eisenstadt [an inn in Vienna much frequented by Schubert and friends], where I remained with Schober, Schubert and Schwind until almost 1 a.m. Needless to say, we talked of nothing but Beethoven, his works and the well-merited honours paid to his memory today.' This was the day of Beethoven's funeral, at which Schubert had been one of the torch-bearers.

Less noted and less discernible is the undoubted influence on Schubert of another contemporary who was then enjoying fame and a high reputation, both as performer and composer: Johann Nepomuk Hummel (1778–1837), whose fields of activity meant that he often crossed paths with Schubert in his early days. The Hungarian-born composer settled in Vienna in 1793 (the same year as Beethoven) and studied composition under Albrechtsberger (who was also Beethoven's teacher). Hummel also had some help from Haydn and advice from Salieri on writing for the theatre. Although he spent much time touring, he was back in Vienna in 1803, was Kapellmeister to Prince Esterházy for a time from 1804, and in 1810 had his opera *Mathilde von Guise* performed at the Kärntnerthor Theater. He was active as a teacher and performer in Vienna between 1811 and 1816, after which he moved to Stuttgart. His music, which many consider facile, nevertheless had a bold melodic charm and individuality that brought it at times very close to the kind of thing that Schubert was writing, and one can connect their ideas at the point where Schubert was trying to write for violin and orchestra. Schubert was a great admirer of Hummel and met him on several occasions. His influence is under-played because Hummel himself is still in need of full recognition.

Moscheles (a pupil of Salieri), Romberg and Ries were contemporaries occasionally in Vienna but worked in different directions from Schubert. Coincidental likenesses between the works of John Field (1782–1837) and Schubert tempt one to suppose a link, but it only seems likely that both were searching for the same romantic goals. The other influence in the field of opera, beside Salieri and Mozart, was Weber (1786–1826), whose advanced romantic ideals must have led Schubert into some of the wrong paths he strayed by during his unsuccessful theatrical flirtations. The outside composer who most influenced Schubert was Rossini, whose Italian operas took Vienna by storm during the most impressionable period of Schubert's life, and whose music added a warm Italian tone to Schubert's music at a period when this was a desirable asset.

The success of Rossini and other Italian composers was often seen as a hindrance to the Germanic composers like Schubert who found difficulty in getting their own operas performed. It had been the same in Mozart's day, when the then popular works of Salieri were to blame. Salieri seems to get blamed for a lot in musical history. William Glock has written: 'The greatest harm Salieri did was to initiate this history of tragic waste, of fine music buried beneath impossible libretti, and of failures that darkened Schubert's days with bitter disappointment.' But that is unfair, and the matter is not quite as straightforward as that. In the first place Salieri had been impressed by some early songs of Schubert's. Salieri had, however, a natural antipathy toward German poetry and tried to persuade Schubert to set such poets as Metastasio, with whom he had written many successes himself. In fact these persuasions had little effect, for Schubert continued to use German literature, both good and bad, as the source of his lyrics. His culture was as deep-rootedly German as Salieri's was Italian (in spite of his fifty years in Germany). Salieri's criticisms of the Mozart operas, still based on old jealousies, had just as little effect, for Schubert continued to worship Mozart and emulate him, except in opera where Salieri's advice might well have helped. Mozart had certainly based some of his greatest successes on Italian libretti and it is surprising that

Schubert did not see *The Marriage of Figaro* as a natural guideline for his own endeavours. Instead he followed the older path of Gluck and relied on third-rate German libretti by his own friends, and pursued a path of operatic failure. The times when Schubert almost achieved an operatic *tour de force* were when he went closest to the conventions of Salieri and Rossini. Salieri offered him an appreciation of the Italian language, so well suited to opera. Even if Schubert did not follow his advice he was still proud to be called 'a pupil of Salieri', as was Beethoven. There must have been more to the man than the jealous villain that is generally implied.

If the greatest influences on Schubert's music were Mozart and Rossini, with Haydn, Hummel and Beethoven of next importance, there was also the music of the day with which he was surrounded. Composers such as Leopold Koželuh (1752–1818), whose rather old-fashioned style Schubert used to admire, preferring him to his successor as Court Musical Director, Franz Krommer (1759–1831) whose music had the same sort of sturdy tunefulness as Hummel's, were highly popular during the last important decade of Schubert's life. There were countless other small streams of influence in the highly musical city of Vienna.

Ultimately, of course, Schubert chose his own path, difficult as it often proved, and in the field where he was to gain most lasting renown – as a songwriter – he was clearly right in his choice of German texts and poets whose works he knew and loved, and who gave him the right sort of emotional stimulus. The young mind is apt to find its excitement in curious quarters, frequently in writers, composers and painters who are not regarded highly by posterity but who wrote in a highly charged and perhaps artificial idiom that was popular at the time. These youthful tastes rarely do any harm and achieve a purpose by providing a stepping-stone to a wider appreciation of the arts. They at least implant the habit of reading, listening or looking. The composer always quoted as a great and lasting influence on Schubert's predilection for song-writing was Johann Rudolf

Zumsteeg, who was born in Baden in 1760 and died in Stuttgart in 1802. He had been a fellow pupil and a friend of the poet Schiller at the Karlschule in Stuttgart. Schiller had a taste for the macabre and indulged with others in the production of somewhat morbid and melodramatic ballads, given respectability by historical and legendary subjects, which Zumsteeg was particularly active in setting (amongst his many other works, both vocal and instrumental). The music of Zumsteeg means nothing today but it was then much admired by Haydn for its 'imagination and fine sense of form'. The young Schubert was greatly drawn to these blood-and-thunder pieces, which were totally Germanic in their dark nastiness and savage emotionalism. They indicated a route away from much of the delicate songwriting of his predecessors. They led to the similar but slightly superior works of such as Goethe, and gave a real basis to at least part of Schubert's most successful endeavours. The Zumsteeg mode was also pursued by other composers from North Germany whose works Schubert probably came across in his formative years. These included Johann Friedrich Reichardt (1752–1814) and Carl Friedrich Zelter (1758–1832), both of whom pursued the same line of picturesque romanticism. Reichardt wrote some seven hundred songs, some of which are highly dramatic, and he must have particularly interested Schubert by his imaginative accompaniments which, almost for the first time in songwriting, had a programmatic intent of their own, suggesting the movement of water or wind in the trees, and attempting some interesting harmonies. He first employed several accompanying patterns that Schubert later found useful. Zelter was a close friend of Goethe, who liked his music and settings above any. This compares with his almost total disregard of Schubert. It is interesting to compare their approach to the same verses.

The world at that time seemed unusually full of songsters and it is mainly Schubert's melodic gift and the complementary rightness of his accompaniments that now sets him above these predecessors and contemporaries in Vienna who were busily writing in answer to the cloistered demands of Biedermeier society. But their names are now mainly forgotten.

Yet, at the time, it was Schubert who seemed to make no headway and remained definitely an outsider to the main musical circles. Even the few musicians who did enter his circle of intimate friends seemed to fail to grasp his greatness. Franz Lachner (1803–90), who studied in Vienna and became assistant conductor at the Kärntnerthor Theater in 1826, and principal conductor after Weigl from 1827–34, became a close friend of Schubert's. He is reported as saying, even long after Schubert was dead and beginning to be recognised, that he thought it a pity that Schubert never learned as much about music as he did; otherwise, with his definite talent, he might also have become a master. Benedikt Randhartinger (1802–93), who went to the same school, sang in the Court Chapel choir from 1832 and was later one of its conductors, said that he was only sorry that Schubert had always remained until the end a bit of a dilettante. This view that Schubert was talented but a perpetual amateur was maintained, by Busoni and others, until late into the nineteenth century. These views were, of course, based on the inadequate knowledge they had of Schubert's actual output, and the quality and depth that the posthumously discovered works reveal.

Knowing that Schubert was there and intensely creative at the time, we may now find a strange void in our distant view of the busy and dedicated musical life of Vienna, at such a time, for instance, as March 1822, when Gioacchino Rossini came to Vienna like a musical god. He was only five years older than Schubert (who had just finished writing his ill-fated *Alfonso und Estrella*) and Vienna had heard and adored eight or so of his operas, including the famous *Il Barbiere di Siviglia* and *La Gazza ladra* in 1819. There had been much scathing criticism of them from the pro-Teutonic, anti-Italian critics, but this had not deterred the public. From April to July 1822 the Kärntnerthor Theater staged a Rossini festival beginning on 13 April with *Zelmira* which lasted four hours but, in the words of one enthusiast, 'does not seem long to anyone, even the musicians, which is saying something'. Rossini's friend Barbaja was in charge at the theatre and most of the performances were enthusiastically and expertly conducted by Josef Weigl, whose own operatic ambitions marked him as a potentially jealous rival of Rossini's. As Rossini himself reported: 'He had been described to me as one of my enemies but, as if to convince me of the contrary, he rehearsed with such care as I have never experienced in myself or anyone else. At times I felt like asking him not to carry his exactness to such extremes; but it all went off wonderfully.' His wife, Isabella Colbran, sang the leading role in this opera and others that were produced such as *La Cenerentola*, *Matilda di Shabran*, *Elisabetta Regina d'Inghilterra*, *La Gazza ladra* and *Ricciardo e Zoraide*. Crowds gathered outside the windows of the rooms where Rossini and Colbran were staying and called for them as if they were royalty. They opened the windows, moved the piano near them and jointly performed an aria from *Elisabetta*, and encores in response to the cries of 'Viva, viva' from the street. Even Rossini himself sang a popular number from *Il Barbiere di Siviglia* before they decided that enough was enough and around midnight retired to bed to a background of disappointed groans from the enthusiasts. They were followed in the street and hailed everywhere until they returned to Italy. Early in April Salieri managed to arrange a meeting with Beethoven. They found the morose composer living in dingy poverty, working at his piano. He congratulated Rossini on *Il Barbieri di Siviglia*, saying that it would be heard as long as Italian opera survived and added the rather barbed comment that Rossini ought only to write *opera buffa* for which his talent was totally suited. Rossini was so moved by the plight of Beethoven that he spent much of his time at subsequent parties with the Viennese establishment trying to persuade them to give the composer a proper pension. But they simply shrugged and said: 'That is the way Beethoven wants it: he is misanthropic and morose and doesn't want friendship.'

And where was Schubert, who worshipped Beethoven from afar, while all this fêting and banqueting was going on? Possibly begging a seat in the gallery from a charitable official at the Kärntnerthor; perhaps, on the way back to his lonely room after a drink at the local inn, amongst the crowd in the street who gazed up adoringly at the celebrated Italian on the balcony. There is no record of Rossini having even heard of him or making any mention of his music, in spite of a generous assessment of other talents that extended as far as the frivolities of Offenbach in later years.

If the years after his death rightly saw a proper reassessment of Schubert as a great and serious musician, the one who most instinctively captured the musical spirit of Vienna in his writings, there is no cause to pour scorn and blame on individuals who failed to realise his talent during his lifetime. Schubert chose to be an outsider to some extent and was ahead of his time; as is the recurring fate of such individual genius. He is most adequately summed up in William Glock's description of his works as 'a perfect fusion of popular and serious music'. Even today the serious musical world can only bring itself to give reluctant lip-service to the role and importance of popular music. In the subsequent earnest and justified desire to prove, in recompense, that Schubert was one of the great classical composers we may be over-inclined to play down the 'popular' side of his genius. Many who knew him at the time might have seen a great deal more of this side of him and very often heard him playing what would be referred to today as 'light' music. Schubert himself, as we know from various contemporary mentions, took every opportunity to hear performances of classical music and the opera. But it is highly likely that he spent an equal amount of time, if not more, enjoying and actively seeking out, in the company of his fun-loving friends, music of a much more frivolous and simplistic nature whose spirit he appreciated and strongly reflected in his own writings. Writers from Deutsch downward understandably underplay this part of his life in their attempts to earn him a respectable reputation. We do know of trips to distant inns to hear folk-singers perform, from which he brought back airs that were incorporated in his own songs and other works. If you were among those who knew enough of Franz Schubert to wish to seek out his company it was to the *Heurigen*, the wine-bars, the coffee-houses that you went, where the composer was intent not only on getting quietly sozzled but also in absorbing the strains of the inevitable music-making. True, he has been reported as rounding, on at least one drunken occasion, on the hack musicians who could not hold a candle to his own talents, but this was only a moment of wine-induced self-revelation and frustration. Schubert was known to be an admirer of the music of Josef Lanner whose orchestra he went to hear whenever he could. And, indeed, we find Schubert active among such composers, contributing to no less than seventeen collections of New Year dance collections (it was already a tribal musical feast in Vienna) such as the one issued by Sauer & Leidesdorf in 1823 where, amongst the contributors of 'original German dances for the Pianoforte', are Czerny, Horzalka, Leidesdorf, Pamer, Payer, Pensel, Pixis, Preisinger, Schoberlechner, Stein, Schubert and Worzischek. These well-used collections are now rarities but they are a firm reminder that the golden age of Viennese dance music, though not yet graced by the presence of the great Johann Strauss II (1825–99), who was still toddling around when Schubert died, was already well into its stride as the Vienna Congress of 1814 took place. Hieronymous Payer was the leader of the orchestra at the Theater an der Wien. Michael Pamer (1782–1827) was the leader of Vienna's most popular dance orchestra which played at the Sperl dance-hall in Rossau, and in its ranks were to be found the elder Johann Strauss (1804–49) and Josef Lanner (1801–43) whose youthful popular talents must have been observed by Schubert on more than one occasion. Lanner and Strauss formed their own orchestra in the 1820s, and Strauss was leading his own by 1825 and had been published by 1827.

The waltz craze hit Vienna from around 1780 and by 1809 dance-halls, ranging from the seedy to the dazzlingly opulent, such as Sperl's, were springing up all over Vienna with their complement of eating and drinking. A German journalist noted all this with amazement in 1809 and hazarded a guess that at least a quarter of the population must have spent their evenings waltzing. The inauguration of one of the grandest of them all, the Apollo Palace, in 1808, was a great social event. Four thousand people were admitted at 25 gulden a head; many more clamoured for entry outside. The opening coincided with the Emperor's wedding. The papers glowed with descriptions of its huge circular dining-hall set about with a hundred round tables and easy chairs; its great polished dance floor flooded with the sound of an invisible orchestra; with artificial grottoes and billiard-rooms available for those who tired of dancing and yearned for other sport. In fact, its excesses led to bankruptcy in 1819 but that was still only the beginning of the great waltz age.

While it is unlikely that Schubert ever whirled round the Apollo, he almost certainly spent a fair proportion of his evenings listening to the Schrammel quartets in the wine-gardens in summer, and might well have been dragged into the world of popular music himself. In truth, he was probably no more at home in this opportunist society than he was in academic circles. His own music in this vein possibly suffered neglect from its very sensitivity and superiority. Certainly no-one, not even Mozart or the great Johann Strauss, ever wrote intrinsically better Viennese waltzes than Schubert. He even wrote one that became what today we might call 'top of the pops', but found it being pirated and exploited by everyone but himself.

If Schubert found that he fitted uncomfortably into the musical world (as someone of comparable talent and inclination would even today), he found more companionable and parallel spirit in the literary world. He was, throughout his life, an avid reader, finding his greatest pleasure in poetry in particular. Literature tends, perhaps, to be a step or two ahead of music in evolutionary spirit and it was there that Schubert found the blossoming of the new romantic era that accorded so well with his own musical ideas. There was a greater kinship there than he could find in his musical predecessors and contemporaries. The best place to consider these literary influences is, of course, in a survey of his song-writing activities in a later chapter. The vastness of his inspired output in this direction leads us to suppose that, to an extent that we can never verify, Schubert was constantly ferreting in libraries and poring over books in order to find the inspirational fodder for his creations. It was thus that Schubert, in one well-known case, found the inspiration for *Die schöne Müllerin.* The musical world is greatly indebted to Wilhelm Müller for this superb song-cycle, as well as *Winterreise.* Müller's book, which contains the sequence of poems *The Fair Maid of the Mill*, was published in 1821. In 1823, so the story goes, Schubert came across the book in the library of his friend Benedikt Randhartinger while he was waiting to see him. Idly browsing through the volume which happened to be lying around, he became so excited by the poems and the musical thoughts that came into his head that he hurried home at once, taking the book with him. The next day, returning to apologise, he showed his friend some of the songs that he had already completed.

III The Man

1 THE IMAGE

If we are not careful, biography tends to blur the image of its subject more than it helps. So often, in the cases of the great composers, the truth seems so hurtful to the aura of their achievement that it is whitewashed by the collusion of forgetfulness that is euphemistically known as the romantic image. To be honest it is not really helpful to know, and therefore we do not want to know, that the greatest composer of all time (I refer, of course, to Mozart) appears to have been mainly occupied (when he was not engaged in the peremptory writing of masterpieces) with rather furtive sex and money problems, with a regular desire to get away from it all in that quiet chapel-of-ease – the billiard room. It becomes a tantalising mystery that all that divinely reassuring music should come from one who has remained so faceless. Nobody has left us a clear image of what he looked like and most of the attributed portraits conflict. The odd reference based on actual contact gives an image of a self-effacing little fellow exhibiting a simple-minded delight in any crumb of praise that was cast his way.

Biography, certainly biography at a distance, much of it based accruing legend, obviously has little to tell about life beyond the public appearance. The details of daily life, and what actually happened at the privacy of the desk, when a Schubert knocked out an immortal song in an hour or so, is not only totally unknown but actually obscured by generations of musicologists telling us that he wrote it in ABBCBA form and giving us details of his chord changes and modulations. At best we can survey the general background and conditions of the creative artist's life and apply a little amateur psychoanalysis in the hope of finding out why he thought and created as he did.

Mozart achieved an output that was not only immense but reasonably orderly and progressive, and of an unfailing high standard; the result of a life that was disrupted by travel, performance and depredation. Schubert produced an erratic, illogical and variable volume of work in the course of a life that seems to have been arrayed in ordinariness. By comparison with almost anyone of comparable genius he was a failure in his lifetime; not a total one, for we can find many tributes to his talent, but certainly in practical terms. His total earnings from his music over twelve years of trying to live on it was in the region of £750. This, of course, is rather more than it sounds. Deutsch reckons that the equivalent in 1925 would have been about £2,000, so the equivalent today would have been around £25,000 – but still little enough to make in a total career and as the results of proven genius. From a list of over 900 works, just over a hundred were published in his lifetime, and most of his major works were completely unknown.

His friends nicknamed him *Schwammerl* ('little mushroom') which is a politely synonymous version of the adjective 'tubby'. There is little to suggest that Schubert radiated an aura of genius or that you would look twice at him if you passed him in the street. The portraits of Mozart have long baffled the world. They offer such a contradictory range of images – from that of a pockmarked, snub-nosed, coarse little fellow to a delicate-featured aesthete (the latter usually preferred in the alabaster busts that proliferate in music shops) – that we are left with no clear idea of the man at all. The Schubert portraits do at least adhere to a common shape and similar features surmounted by the inevitable ill-fitting spectacles, but even so, when we look at them intently and try to draw the personality from the page, there are small but disturbing differences. Portrait-painting is a precarious art at the best of times. One wrong line can ruin an almost perfect likeness, for the personal image is the result of such fine and infinite variation. Schubert sat for no truly great painter. Most of his portrayers were simply artistic friends; but we are indebted to them for a remarkable number of paintings and sketches covering such a brief life and one of such limited contemporary fame. Otto Deutsch, in his large documentary work, comments on the portraits that he considered authentic, helped by the opinions of those who knew Schubert. Deutsch, with the backing of Schwind, Sonnleithner and others, suggests that the sepia water-colour by Wilhelm August Rieder done in 1825 (and signed by Schubert) was the best portrait of all (Rieder had met Schubert in 1823 and became a close friend). It was engraved by Passini in the same year and lithographed by Rieder himself in 1828, also serving for the lithograph by Clarot used by Diabelli & Co. from 1826. Sonnleithner wrote that it was

> the most like him, though the body is too heavy and broad. Schubert was below average height [generally reckoned at around 5 ft 1 in.], had a round, fat face, a short neck and not too high a forehead, a mass of brown and naturally curly hair, round shoulders and back, chubby arms and hands with short fingers – and, if I remember rightly, grey-blue eyes. Bushy brows, nose short and wide and thick lips; his face was rather Moorish. His skin was more fair than dark though minor rashes reddened it occasionally. His head was hunched between his shoulders and pushed forward. He always wore glasses. His expression was obtuse more than intellectual and inclined to be sullen. Only if he was observed more closely while listening to music or engaged in interesting conversation did his face become more alive, his mouth more smiling, his eyes sparkling and his whole posture more relaxed.

As we might fear, this leads us to the conclusion that Schubert, like most composers, was anything but a beauty and might even have been of a slightly boorish, as well as Moorish, aspect. Sonnleithner's words match the Rieder drawing fairly well; but this tack is pursued to extremes by the later Leroux drawing which we frequently see and which somehow manages to emphasise the alcoholic side of his nature. Joseph von Spaun also liked the Rieder portrait and saw it as improving the Schubert image:

> Schubert has up to now been incorrectly depicted in body and spirit. His face is painted like an ugly negro's though everyone who knew him must contradict this. The portrait painted by Rieder is extremely like him. Look and see whether his face is ugly or negroid. It cannot be claimed that Schubert was beautiful but he was well-built and whenever he spoke or smiled or was full of enthusiasm or aglow with passion, his features then seemed noble and almost beautiful.

In spite of this, Kreissle von Hellborn still wrote in 1865 that Schubert 'was anything but attractive' and had 'a round and puffy face, low forehead, projecting lips, bushy eyebrows, stumpy nose, and short curly hair, that gave him that negro look which corresponds with that conveyed by the bust which is to be found at the Währing churchyard'.

As with Mozart, there is little to support the romanticised image of Schubert that admirers felt was his due in the years after his death. A drawing *c.* 1807 of an Imperial Court choirboy by Leo Deit could well be of Schubert but this cannot be confirmed. He was, after all a leading light at the school and the doughy face has something of him in it. Deutsch states that no portrait by his close friend Moritz von Schwind exists beyond the small figure in the famous 'Game of Ball at Atzenbrugg' (*c.* 1820). The catalogue of the 1978 Vienna Schubert exhibition, however, has two portraits by Schwind, one being Schubert at 16, c. 1813. The likeness to his step-mother Anna, also portrayed by Schwind at his home in similar style, is strange and remarkable. The other is *c.* 1820 where he has become plumper and slightly more Germanic. Schwind liked the profile angle and kept fairly faithfully to the small turned-up nose and lowish forehead image (together with those rather ineffective-looking glasses). The various drawings in which Schubert is but a small cartoon keep the owlish and slightly comical image intact: a family drawing by brother Carl Schubert (presumably made *c.* 1822); an anonymous silhouette (for once without the glasses which he had worn from around 1814) dated 1817; Kupelwieser's 'Excursion of the Schubertians' painted for Schober in 1820 (a tiny image), and likewise the 'Party Game of the Schubertians', also painted for Schober by Kupelwieser in 1821; and the amusing little cartoon probably drawn by Schober *c.* 1825, with Michael Vogl and Franz Schubert 'setting out to fight and conquer', where Schubert is decidedly comical and his small stature cruelly emphasised against Vogl's towering height.

The more detailed portraits include those by Kupelwieser in 1821, a full-face drawing in pencil which produced a somewhat confusing image (largely because of the unusually long delineation of the nose and the greater prominence of the eyes); the detail from Kupelwieser's 'Party Game' drawing has a similar receding head and chin effect in profile which seems to put this artist slightly out of line with the rest. Teltscher's 1826 lithograph, however, gets back to the pug-nosed, squinting-eyed, sensuous-lipped image and has quite an air of authenticity about it (if we are to back personal hunches). This is not too well supported by the group drawing of Jenger, Anselm Hüttenbrenner and Schubert made by Teltscher around 1827, in which his view of Schubert seems to have shifted by now more toward the bucolic, with Schubert looking like a typically debauched Dylan Thomas which, perhaps by this time, was the direction in which he was inclining. The image again has a ring of truthfulness about it. One hesitates to contradict those who knew Schubert but we are free to feel (or to hope) that Schubert was more as Teltscher saw him than Rieder's Moorish impression.

The tendency toward the romanticising and alabastering of Schubert, in common with all other musical portraits, naturally gained momentum after his death but had already begun by the end of his life. The last portrait done within his lifetime was that usually (but apparently wrongly) attributed to Willibrord Josef Mähler in 1827, commissioned for Josef Sonnleithner's collection of musicians' portraits. Our reliance on contemporary memory after the commendation of the Rieder portrait is slightly shaken by the view that the Mähler portrait was also very successful. The painter confuses us right away by tactfully removing the ever-present spectacles. Having done so, however, he draws a clear-eyed fellow with highish forehead and a healthy look that not only contradicts Schubert's personal history but also the previous portraits. Already we are beginning to see Schubert as we would perhaps have liked to see him; a likeness to some extent, but with a little of the sweet wholesomeness that geniuses ought to radiate discreetly painted in. Reliance on Mähler, anyway, is totally shattered by a posthumous painting he did of Schubert which (although very much based on the Rieder portrait with a different body posture) returns his glasses but so glamorises the rest (by a face-lift on his nose and brows) that we are suddenly in the presence of the hero of the Schubert-based operetta *Lilac Time* – a highly romanticised image to say the least. The bust produced for Schubert's grave in the Währing cemetery in 1829 produces an unlifelike distortion of the image into which a bit of Beethoven (not inappropriately in view of his proximity) appears to be creeping. Were we not told that it is supposed to be Schubert we might not guess. If the sculptor had access to his subject, or had known Schubert, could this be yet another side of him? Safer perhaps to assume it to be an imaginative figment by a monumental sculptor.

After his death the Schubert legend, in word and painting, began the usual course of distortion that fond memory produces. Nearly all 'coffee-table' books on Schubert carry a beautiful Keats-like drawing by Kupelwieser, firmly underlined with such captions as 'Schubert aged 16'. Deutsch firmly denies that the drawing is even by Kupelwieser or that the drawing, done before the artist knew his subject, was ever intended to be the composer. The doe-eyed, beauteous youth it offers is undoubtedly what the composer of so much heavenly music ought to look like, but it conflicts violently with the snub-nosed choirboy that others saw mooching moodily around Vienna at the time. A miniature by Theer and a portrait by Kettner are likewise summarily dismissed by Deutsch. After his death the heroic statue with Churchillian chin that graces the Stadtpark, perpetually drawing inspiration from the Viennese air, was only to be expected. After all, a round-shouldered, five-foot dwarf with squinting eyes behind crooked glasses and riddled with venereal disease and alcoholism would hardly have been acceptable to the tastes of the time. It is fascinating, if confusing, to compare the description by Georg Franz Eckel (who was at school with Schubert) written in 1858 (thirty years after the composer's death) with Sonnleithner's frank account quoted above. The occasional contradictions are intriguing:

> The figure short but sturdy, with well-developed solid bones and firm muscles; not angular but rather rounded. The neck short and strong; shoulders, chest and pelvis broad, finely curved; arms and thighs rounded; hands and feet small; his walk lively and vigorous. The fairly large, round and powerful skull was surrounded by brown, abundant hair. The face, in which the forehead and chin were particularly well developed, showed traits that were not so much actually beautiful as expressive and forceful. The mild eyes, brown if I remember rightly, which could flash fire when excited, were overshadowed by prominent and bushy brows and thus seemed smaller than they really were, especially as he tended to narrow them as short-sighted people do. His nose was of medium size, blunt and tilted up a little with a gentle inward sweep to his full and thick though firmly set lips which he generally kept closed. His chin was deeply dimpled. His complexion was pale but vital, as is usual with genius. The liveliness of his features mirrored the creative impulses within, stern-looking if he frowned and compressed his lips, sweet-natured when he smiled and his eyes shone. Altogether Schubert's expression showed an Olympian's classic expression of balance between vigour and calm.

Schubert solidly refuted, in most of the accounts we have of him, the romantic conception of the heroic genius, the creator whose glorious works arose from a matching glory of thought, action and appearance. Most people found Schubert an ordinary little man and one of his friends, Moritz von Schwind, when called upon in later years to describe what he looked like, summed him up with the telling phrase: 'Like a drunken cabby!' A German admirer, the poet and folklorist Heinrich Hoffmann, who went to Vienna in 1827 with a friend in the hopes of meeting Schubert (whom he had worshipped from afar) not only found Schubert doing his best not to meet him and ignoring all invitations but, when he did bump into him accidentally in a Grinzing bar, had nothing to say and hurriedly left. Hoffmann was bitterly disappointed at such ill-manners and lack of human grace – a person who bore no resemblance to the Schubert he had admiringly imagined. Other acquaintances variously described him as 'a Bavarian peasant', 'anything but striking or prepossessing', 'as undistinguished as a man as he was distinguished as a composer' and 'of wooden appearance'.

It is difficult to rid those who have not met poets and painters, writers and composers, of the conception that all great creative artists must also be great and profound men, or that the aura of genius radiates from them with a glowing light. The action of creation is not a matter of personality or character. It is often the lesser artist who builds a flamboyant reputation on charm, wit and appearance. The creation of music itself is a less exalted activity than many commentators and surmisers would have us believe. It is, after all, the placement of chords and notes in an effective order, partly mathematical. The difference between doing it effectively or dully is simply a matter of imagination, an inner motivation that can be hidden behind the dullest facade. These same commentators are apt to go to the other extreme and declare that a composer like Schubert was merely a spider spinning webs intuitively and without knowledge. The experiment in his work and his occasional utterances also refute this view. He was intelligent, perceptive and imaginative and, of course, he was not altogether a boor. He loved company and he enjoyed a convivial drinking life with his friends, who were by no means all involved in music; he could be warm and amusing. But mainly he led a quiet, inner life, intently writing, starting a new work the moment another was finished, unwilling and unable to move in fashionable society and, of course, inevitably coming up against the disadvantages of such a personality and attitude. He did not impress society, as many lesser artists did, he was unable to obtain lucrative posts, and he found that genius was not enough in a world that judges by appearances. Most of the time he was melancholic and unhappy, and such a state does not help friendship or co-operation. The limited fame and localised repute that came to him was by way of individual recognition of his abilities and unaided by the added lustre that the cult of personality can bring. The world at large knew little of his art. Edward Holmes, visiting Vienna in 1827 to study music and musicians, makes no mention of Schubert in the book he wrote in 1828. The first book about Schubert, by Kreissle von Hellborn, did not appear until 1865 and, even then, much of his music was still neglected. And yet, paradoxically, we are not in any great ignorance of Schubert's life and creative activities. Compared to what we know of Mozart, there is a great richness of detail that comes out through the loving memories of his family and friends; even if none of them seemed to have quite realised what stature of genius was amongst them.

Although Schubert is often and rightly acclaimed as the only truly great composer who was actually a native of Vienna (and consequently an essentially Viennese quality is often attributed to his music), his immediate ancestry, only one generation back, was Moravian. Moravia, under Hapsburg control from early in the seventeenth century, was a crown land of Austria, its boundaries some eighty or so miles north of Vienna. In 1849 it became a separate province and in 1918 found its true alliance as part of Czechoslovakia. Something of the spirit of the Moravian dance can be found in Schubert. Earlier the family had come from Styria, to the south-west of Vienna and the province of Austria, the end of the alpine region that stretched west through Salzburg and Tyrol. The Tyrolean element is within his music too. To Vienna's immediate east lies Hungary, in Schubert's day all a part of the great Austro-Hungarian empire with all that its cultural legacy implies. Vienna simply became a centre of all these cultural strains, the linking element coming from Germany in the person of such composers as Hummel and Beethoven, the latter very much the shaping element of Schubert's more formal music.

2 EARLY DAYS

The background to Schubert's arrival into this troubled world has a depressingly Dickensian mixture of morbidity and genteel poverty about it. No doubt there was much family happiness and togetherness, some of it occasioned by a love of music, but it was a struggling lower middle-class existence that was scarcely conducive to soaring thoughts. Schubert's grandfather Karl was a Moravian peasant farmer who achieved some respectability as a senior juror (a sort of local magistrate) in Neudorf. He had thirteen children, four of whom survived into adulthood. One of these was the eldest son Karl, born in 1755, who renounced farming and went to Vienna where he became a schoolteacher. Schubert's father, Franz Theodor Florian, probably born around 1759–60 (though other dates have been given) had similar scholastic leanings. After six years in the grammar school at Brünn and three years as an assistant teacher in local schools he went to Vienna, where he hoped to study philosophy, and joined his brother Karl as an assistant at his school in the Leopoldstadt suburb of Vienna.

At some time and place (the details are unknown) he met a girl called Elisabeth Vietz, the daughter of a locksmith from Zuckmantel in Silesia. At the time she was working in domestic service as a cook in Vienna. They were married in January 1875 (the certificate gives his age as twenty-five, hers as twenty-eight) and settled down in his lodgings in Liechtental at 152 Brunngasse (now 20 Badgasse). Their first child, by some fluke (in view of subsequent attempts)a survivor, Ignaz, was born in March 1785. Their continued attempts at rearing children proceeded disastrously but do not seem to have proved discouraging. High infant mortality was very much the norm of the time amongst poorer families. There was Elisabeth (b. 1786) who lived for just over two years; Karl (1787) who lived for less than a year; Franziska Magdalena (1788) - three months; another Franziska Magdalena (1789) - two and a half years; Franz Karl (1790) - one month; Anna Karoline (1791) - eighteen days; Petrus (1792) - six months; and Josef (1793) who lived to the ripe old age of five. Their second real success came only with Ferdinand Lukas (1794), followed by Franz Karl (1795).

During this sad period a number of events, domestic and universal, had occurred. In June 1786, Franz Theodor was appointed, being accounted a good teacher and an upright character, as schoolmaster at 12 (now 3) Säulengasse in the Himmelpfortgrund in a house called 'Zum schwarzen Rosel' ('The Black Horse').

At some unspecified date, but probably around 1796, the Schuberts and their surviving brood, at the time Ignaz, Josef and Ferdinand, moved to the Himmelpfortgrund, taking up residence at No. 72 in the Upper High Street (Hauptstrasse von der Nussdorfer Linie), now known as 54 Nussdorferstrasse, in a lodging house, owned by one Matthias Schmidtgruber, known as 'Zum roten Krebsen' ('The Red Crayfish'). The house, originally made up of sixteen small apartments on the ground and first floors (each consisting of one big room and one small), had been apportioned more generously between half a dozen families and the Schuberts rented what had originally been two apartments.

The school occupied two large ground-floor rooms and was so short of space and so ill-equipped that its 180 pupils had to attend in two groups, half in the morning and half in the afternoon. Nor was the appointment, more of a licence, any great privilege. The schoolmaster was forced to teach the children of the poor for nothing and left to extract what fees he could from more affluent parents in order to pay his assistants and run the school. When grandfather Karl died in 1787, the whole of a small inheritance disappeared in trying to fit out the school adequately and in paying the rent. Some money still had to be borrowed. Franz stuck to his task assiduously and achieved a gradual improvement of standards and income. But poverty reigned and the raising of children must have seemed a thankless and hopeless task. Leopold tried on several occasions to improve his lot by applying for better schoolmastering posts but always without success.

It was at that house in Himmelpfortgrund that the twelfth child of the marriage, Franz Peter, was born on 31 January 1797 at 1.30 p.m. in, according to Schubert's sister Maria (b. 1801) writing in 1865, what was more or less an alcove, probably one of the smaller rooms normally used as a kitchen and overlooking the courtyard, with its fountain.* Schubert was baptised, as a Catholic, by the Reverend Wanzka at the Liechtenthal parish church (which could be seen from the end of the Schubert's garden) on 1 February. Uncle Karl acted as godfather. With such a record of early deaths in the family, we may count ourselves as fortunate that Franz Peter survived at all. Perhaps the family fortunes were improving by then and meals were more substantial.

Details of Schubert's childhood, his predilections and promises, are virtually nonexistent. He was, we imagine, a stocky but rather unathletic boy, bookishly inclined. Although shortsighted from an early age, his body, when exhumed, had a fine set of undamaged teeth and a thick head of hair and little sign, in general, of vitamin deficiency. Schubert would hardly have been affected by the death of his brother Josef in October 1798 nor by the birth of Aloisia Magdalena on 17 December 1799, who died next day.

By May 1801 Franz Schubert senior had saved enough money

*Schubert's birthplace, with commemorative tablet and bust, became a Schubert museum in 1912, maintained on the first floor by the City of Vienna.

to pay his official levy for the cost of defending Vienna against Napoleon as well as to take on the lease of the 'Black Horse' schoolhouse at a yearly cost of 45 Kreuzer, payable to the Imperial and Royal Estate of Himmelpforte (who had bought it from its previous owner) plus five florins rent per annum. The settling of the fees and the rest of the legal rigmarole makes it likely that the Schuberts at last moved into their own house and school by the autumn of 1801. They could now run it as a proper family concern. Ignaz (a frail, scholarly looking youth) continued there as assistant schoolmaster after his own education was completed. By the time that Franz Schubert started to attend around 1803, Ignaz would have been about seventeen and it was he who took on the budding composer's musical education. But not for long. In a very short time Ignaz was reporting: 'I was very astonished when, after only a few months, he told me he no longer needed any further tuition from me, and that he now wanted to manage by himself. And within a short space of time he made such progress that I was obliged to recognise him as a master who had far surpassed me and whose standard I could no longer acclaim.' Franz senior had also done all he could to encourage all his sons to take an interest in music. He had taught them all to play the violin and read music, and many pleasant evenings were spent playing quartets and other chamber music with the young Franz very much in charge and soon writing pieces for the others to play. Not that the family crush was particularly helpful to the task of composing, particularly when Uncle Karl died in 1804 and Franz senior temporarily accommodated his family of three.

His father and family could have little doubt that the small and tubby Franz was a potential genius by the age of ten. He was first soprano in the local church, a gifted interpreter of everything that he played and sang, including violin solos at special services, and a stream of apprentice works – songs, quartets and piano pieces – was already appearing. The choirmaster Michael Holzer, a hearty drinker, who tried to teach him singing, violin and piano, had to admit, as Ignaz had done, that he was far outstripped: 'Whenever I wished to impart something new to him, he always knew it already. I often looked at him in silent wonder.' This was reported by Schubert's brother Ferdinand, who was to become the one most intimately concerned with Franz's career and well-being. A portrait by his nephew shows Ferdinand as a kindly looking, generous-mouthed, warm-eyed fellow who was taught at the family school and the I. & R. Secondary School in Vienna, and then became assistant teacher to his father in 1810 and a fully qualified teacher in 1816. He was also trained as a musician, taught by Michael Holzer and became leading soprano and soloist in the Liechtenthal church. Later he studied organ and composition with Joseph Drechsler.

Franz senior, astonished by his youngest son's precocity, waited for the first chance to combine his talents with further educational opportunity. It came in 1808 when the *Wiener Zeitung* of 3 August 1808 carried the following advertisement:

> At the end of the present school-year the post for a soprano will fall vacant at the I. &. R. Seminary. Whosoever wishes to obtain this place for his son or ward is to prove to the directorate of the said seminary, where an examination is to be on 1st October, at 9 a.m., that the candidate is fit to enter the first Latin class, possesses a good voice, and has been well instructed in singing.

Schubert and his father duly attended, with Schubert arrayed for the occasion in a very light blue, almost white, coat that seems to have induced some mirth in the other children who dubbed him 'the miller's son' – a prophetic association. He not only impressed them but also the examiners, the court music directors, Antonio Salieri and Josef Eybler, and choirmaster Philipp Körner, and was one of three boys admitted to the Konvikt as choristers of the Chapel of the Imperial Court a week later. The parting with his family was made a little less hard by the excitements of donning his new school uniform – a brown coat with one epaulet, white breeches, shoes with shiny buckles and a three-cornered hat with gold braid. Schubert always enjoyed dressing well, when funds allowed, and as an adult most of his worldly possessions were clothes. A drawing of such a student of the period is assumed to be Schubert himself, but without any real confirmation.

He began a fairly bleak period of five years at the Konvikt which was typical, and still often is, of the prison-like routine attached to becoming a chorister, with school lessons all day and music lessons in the evening, when not actually rehearsing or performing in the Chapel Royal. He was rarely allowed home and contact with his family was restricted to wistful gazes during the course of his public duties when they came to hear him. The school was cold and austere and the food was bad, so that chill and hunger became the usual background to music-making. Schubert appears to have enjoyed the actual indulgences in music and he got good reports from his teachers. He spent what little spare time he had composing and practising in deserted rooms. During work hours he played in the school orchestra and became familiar with the symphonies of Haydn and Mozart (the G minor being amongst his favourites), with occasional and influential sorties into the modern difficulties of Beethoven. He also played in chamber ensembles and gradually learned his craft as a composer by emulation. His teachers, being of the old-fashioned school, did not help him much in this respect. The flow of music that he composed earned him early recognition amongst his fellow-pupils and teachers, and many of his early works had their first (and often last) performances during his lifetime at the school. At the end of the second term his report read: 'Morals – Good; Studies – Good; Singing – Very Good; Violin – Very Good; Pianoforte – Very Good; Remarks – a special musical talent.' The principal music teacher was Wenzel Ruzicka, court organist and a viola player from the Burg Theater, who taught piano, organ, viola, cello and occasionally (with exceptional pupils like Schubert) composition. He also founded the school orchestra and conducted it. Occasionally Schubert was allowed to take over and to conduct his own compositions. In this respect Ruzicka proclaimed that Schubert appeared to have 'learned his art from God'. So there was no lack of recognition of his early talent.

Although he was always of a retiring and solitary disposition when his mind was on composition, Schubert throughout his life exhibited a contrasting convivial side to his nature when he enjoyed the company of friends, the making of music and the strengthening of his courage pleasantly enhanced (in later years) by plenty of hard drinking. Many of his friends, some of them originally from the grammar school of the Kremsmunster Seminary in Upper Austria, played in the school orchestra of some thirty players, and remained loyal to him throughout his life. Georg Franz Eckel, for instance, who played the flute, later became a famous veterinarian and surgeon, and remembered Schubert as 'shy and uncommunicative', spending most of his leisure hours in the music room alone and, on the school outings, 'walking thoughtfully along with lowered eyes and hands behind his back, completely absorbed in his own thoughts'. Another friend was Josef von Spaun, who led the orchestra and took a special interest in Schubert when he found him so wholeheartedly absorbed in music. Spaun, who was older than Schubert, soon left to study law. But he returned to Vienna two years later and immediately renewed the acquaintance, finding Schubert now leading the orchestra and composing prolifically. Schubert's reports on the musical side remained good, though he fell short in subjects like Latin and mathematics. The meagre existence continued to prove arduous and in 1812, in his fourth year, he wrote to his brother Ferdinand a typical schoolboy letter:

> Can I say at once what is on my mind and come to the point rather than beat around the bush. While I have always found my life here passably good there is still much room for improvement. You must know how hungry one can get after an inadequate dinner and only a miserable supper to look forward to over eight hours later always longing for a roll or an

> apple or two. It is my continual need and longing, but the few pence that father is able to allow are all spent in the first few days of the week. What can I do for the rest of the time? Those who put their trust in Thee shall surely not be disappointed. (Matthew Chapter 3, Verse 4.) I believe the same. What would you think of letting me have a few Kreutzers each month. You wouldn't really miss them while I should be happy and resigned to my cloistered life. I refer again to the Apostle Matthew who said: He that hath two coats let him give one to he who has none. Meanwhile, I hope you will listen to the voice that incessantly calls to you – Your loving, poor, hopeful, once more poor – and not to be forgotten brother, Franz.

Whether Ferdinand responded adequately we know not, but life was to change. In May 1812 their mother Elisabeth died of typhus (the disease that was to claim Franz later) aged 55 at 10 Himmelpfortgrund. Franz senior now became the sole lessee of the school and premises. The loss brought father and son close together for a while. The elder Franz had always been a little uneasy about his son's desire to live as a professional musician and would have liked to see him settling down to school-teaching. Matters were temporarily settled in July 1812 when Schubert's voice broke and he had to leave the Court Chapel Choir. His father agreed that he could stay at the school for another year and continue his musical studies if he would apply himself to bringing his academic studies up to the required standards. At the same time Kapellmeister Antonio Salieri himself agreed to take on Schubert as his special pupil. Schubert went twice a week to study harmony and counterpoint with the venerable master and they got on well together. Schubert was ever pleased to call himself 'a pupil of Salieri' and Salieri was proud to proclaim the genius of his pupil. 'He knows everything there is to know about music,' he is reported to have said.

This last year with Salieri proved a fruitful one, for Schubert was now writing such mature works as the song *Der Jüngling am*

Bache ('The youth by the brook'), a Fantasia for Piano Duet, several string quartets, and his first symphony which was dedicated to the head of the Konvikt, Dr Lang, as a leaving gift and played by the school orchestra. During this year Schubert developed his lasting love of opera, and his burning desire to write it, when he went along with Spaun to hear Gluck's *Iphigénie en Tauride* (with Michael Vogl, later to be an influential Schubert acquaintance, singing the baritone role). After the performance they met and had supper with the young poet Theodor Körner, then making a name in the theatre and full of a patriotic fire that made Schubert a firm admirer. Körner further endeared himself by urging Schubert to remain true to himself and not to pander to the persuasions of fashion and academic conventions. Gluck intrigued Schubert in spite of his old-fashioned style (much vaunted by Salieri), and Schubert was soon to find more excitement and influence in the operas of Rossini, just beginning to make their mark in distant Venice, arriving in Vienna some four years later. Körner was soon to be killed in the wars and Schubert ardently set many of his poems to music. Schubert was deeply aware of the struggles of the Austro-Hungarian Empire and the troubled background to life in Vienna. He wrote a song to celebrate a victory in Leipzig in 1813.

With all this composition, music-making and concert-going, the standards in Latin and mathematics made no noticeable improvement, but Salieri and his other teachers were more concerned to see that Schubert continued in his musical studies. Schubert was offered a scholarship on the authority of the Emperor Francis himself, but as the conditions put musical studies at the bottom of the list of requirements, Schubert decided to please his father and himself by agreeing to become an assistant teacher at the family school, by now doing well. There was a great family celebration which included Franz Schubert's new wife Anna Kleyenböck (whom he married a year after Elisabeth's death) and, in October, Schubert wrote a special cantata for his father's nameday. The understanding was that he would be allowed to compose and indulge in musical activities in return for pursuing his duties as a teacher after a year's training at the Normal College. When this was finished Schubert took over the junior class (the school now had over 300 pupils) while Ignaz and Ferdinand were also on the staff. Schubert loathed the work and was poorly rewarded by a token salary of some £8 a year. However, he got on well with his stepmother, who often gave him some of her house-keeping money, and he was to live at the family home for the next three years, until autumn 1816. His schoolmastering duties seemed to handicap him very little, leaving considerable time for composing. During those three years he must have turned out well over the 400 or so items that are officially listed in the Deutsch catalogue, including his first four symphonies, five operas, string quartets, masses and the rest of his output in over 350 songs that gradually found their true style. He composed naturally and fluently, and was known at times to write as many as eight songs in a day, starting another as soon as one was completed. It in no way lessened their worth. He continued to study fitfully with Salieri and began to enjoy musical evenings with his old schoolfriends, who admired his music and did all they could to promote its cause.

September 1814 had seen the settling of European problems and the illustrious Vienna Congress where many new national boundaries were decided. There was temporary cause for optimism. In the spring of the following year Beethoven's revised *Fidelio* was produced at the Theater an der Wien and Schubert sold a few of his school books in order to buy a ticket. He heard all the Beethoven he could and modelled much of his own symphonic writings on those of the great modern master. No doubt he would have liked to have made the acquaintance of his fellow citizen but shyness prevented a meeting with Beethoven, who was unaware of the challenging genius. On the occasions when Schubert passed the surly master in the street he would stare humbly and admiringly but dared make no approach.

Schubert fell in love with Therese Grob, the young daughter of a widowed friend of the family who sang the soprano part on his mass in F when it was performed in the church in Liechtenthal. But he was in no financial position to marry. The affair lingered on a while, with not much response from Therese's side and in 1820 she married a wealthy baker. He had his first success with his setting of Goethe's *Gretchen am Spinnrade* ('Margaret at the spinning-wheel') which he wrote in October 1814. It passed around amongst his acquaintances and was frequently sung at amateur concerts, though not published until 1821 or heard in a professional performance until 1823. Later Heuberger was to describe it as 'the first modern German song'; but to Schubert it was simply a quiet experiment. His contemporaries clearly admired Schubert's music but they were not at all sure of his quirks and very individual styling. They were no doubt often alarmed at his sudden modulations and journeys to strange keys. His songs, among them many more settings of Goethe, found no immediate acceptance in the world of easy drawing-room ballads and *bel canto*. The first song he was to have published was *Erlkönig* in 1821 (on a sale or return basis) and even the manuscript of this was returned by mistake to a hack composer of the same name who lived in Dresden and who was incensed at having such rubbish connected with his reputation. The songs were new in style and approach and (a point always difficult to equate with our own acceptance and admiration) they sounded defiantly modern and intellectual to those brought up on Mozart and lesser Viennese establishment composers.

3 THE EMERGENT COMPOSER

In April 1816, nearing twenty and weary of teaching infants, he now decided to leave the family school and applied for a post as music master in Laibach. But he failed to get the appointment, in spite of a glowing testimony from Salieri. Celebrating the old composer's fiftieth year in Vienna, he wrote a cantata. He was actually paid for another cantata that he wrote for a friend of Spaun and noted in his diary for 17 June 1816, with a hint of pride, 'I composed today for the first time for money. Namely a cantata, words by Dräxler, for Prof. Wattrot's name-day. The fee is 100 Viennese florins.' Aside from his practical view of life, Schubert was also something of an amateur philosopher, and his diary entry for September 1816 muses on a Shakespeare quotation which he vaguely remembered about 'All the world's a stage. . . .' and the individual's luck in getting the right part or not. More practical thoughts follow about the happiness of finding a true friend and the terrifying though tempting prospect of marriage. Therese Grob was obviously haunting his mind. Elsewhere his diary reflects his regular love of walking in the country.

Another figure who came into Schubert's life at this time was Franz von Schober, a fellow medical student friend of Spaun's. He came from a rich family, with a German father and a Viennese mother, who lived an unconventional intellectual family life. Schober was something of an adventurer but, strangely, he was liked by both Schubert and Spaun. From the spring of 1816 Schubert had left home to stay temporarily with Spaun. In autumn 1816 he was persuaded to lodge in the Schober household at what was then 592 Inner City (where 26 Tuchlauben now stands). It was a fruitful move, for it was Schober who introduced Schubert to Michael Vogl, the singer he had heard and admired in Gluck's opera. It was an embarrassed meeting at first, for Vogl was much older than Schubert, nearing fifty and famous, but he agreed to try one of Schubert's songs and conceded that it was 'not bad'. In fact he soon became a great champion of Schubert's music and did much to help him become known in Vienna. Yet another influential person Schubert met around the 1816–17 period was the poet Johann Mayrhofer, who brought him into contact with a group of idealists with whom he edited a literary magazine, led by Johann Senn (who had also been a fellow student at the Imperial College). By 1817 Schubert was writing fewer songs but amongst those he did write were some of an immediately attractive nature, such as *Die Forelle* ('The Trout') and *An die Musik* and some popularly dramatic pieces like *Der Tod und das Mädchen* ('Death and the Maiden'). He was turning more to instrumental and orchestral music by now and was working on his Fourth Symphony which he conceived in the 'grand' unified style of Beethoven. He managed to have it rehearsed at the private musical meetings held in the house of a music-loving lawyer Leopold von Sonnleithner, who ran a small amateur orchestra, and it was played in 1818 at the home of the orchestral leader Otto Hatwig. With the help of such influential friends his music, still regarded as daring and experimental, began to circulate in Vienna. Some operas of Rossini had now become known in Vienna* and much influenced Schubert. An *Overture in the Italian Style* (which one is uncertain) was the work heard at the first professional performance of any of Schubert's music. This was on 1 March 1818 at a public concert organised by Eduard Jaëll (the first violinist of the Hatwig orchestra) at the Gasthof Zum Römischen Kaiser. One of his songs was published in an almanack and public performances of his works became reasonably regular with a few favourable notices ensuing. Requests came in regularly for partsongs and masses for the use of amateur choral societies. By the end of 1818 he had been offered employment as music master during the summer months to the two young daughters of Count Esterhäzy to whom he had been introduced by the singer Karl Unger. The small regular income would be welcome and Schubert took his first long journey outside Vienna, some 100 miles to Zseliz. He led a fairly leisurely life enlivened by flirtations with a pretty lady's maid called Pepi Pöckelhofer whom he occasionally saw later in Vienna. The easy life was, as so often happens, not conducive to composition, which was mainly confined to writing piano duets for his young pupils. He began to tire of his refined life and longed to return to his working and drinking haunts in Vienna. The opportunity came when the Esterhäzy family took up their winter residence in the city. He now had a commission for a one-act opera (after many futile attempts to get one accepted) for the Court Theatre.

* The first Rossini opera to be staged in Vienna was *L'Inganno felice*, at the Kärntnerthor Theater in 1816, followed by *Tancredi* (1816), *L'Italiana in Algeri* (1817), *Ciro in Babalonia* (1817), etc.

He finished the delightful farcical piece *Die Zwillingsbrüder* in two months and was paid around fifty pounds for his labours. It was not actually staged until 1820 and, before it was, Schubert had already been commissioned to write the music of a full-length piece called *Die Zauberharfe*. It produced one of his masterpieces, an overture which later came in handy in connection with *Rosamunde*. He did not return with the Esterhäzy family to their summer residence in 1819 but instead took a trip into the Austrian countryside to spend a summer holiday in Steyr, having established a *pied à terre* in Vienna in what was then 420 Inner City, sharing lodgings with Johann Mayrhofer. His companion on the trip was Michael Vogl. Schubert stayed with an old school friend, Albert Stadler and, with a little money in his pocket, and the companionship of the four pretty daughters of the house-owner, a lawyer called Schellmann, it proved a pleasantly rosy period of his life. There was a flourishing local music society, led by one Sylvester Paumgartner (a gifted amateur cellist who managed the local iron works), for which he wrote an inspired Piano Quintet. Within their ranks was Pepi von Koller, daughter of a leading merchant who was a brilliant pianist and a good bass player. The format was thus more or less decided for him and when Schubert, Paumgartner and Vogl discussed the andantino variation movement, Schubert gladly accepted Paumgartner's suggestion that it should be based on the song they all loved, *Die Forelle*. The country air, the good company and the wine made this a very happy holiday, which also inspired one of his most lyrically Schubertian Piano Sonatas in A major (D 664) written for Pepi. These he polished and completed on his return to Vienna. The search for ever-elusive happiness and its realisation in such carefree moments was expressed in his setting of a poem by Schiller later that year: '*Schöne Welt, wo bist du?*' (D677).

Back in Vienna he started his fine Mass in A flat (D 678). Yet 1820 was to be a disturbed year in which Schubert, through his various political and intellectual friendships, was to come closest to brushes with the authorities, for which he had no taste or desire. The philosophers Schelling and Schlegel were viewed with suspicion by the authorities and Schubert's friend Franz Bruchmann was almost arrested because he went to Erlangen, without a permit, to hear Schelling speak. Schubert had been lodging with Johann Mayrhofer since autumn 1818 in his third-floor flat at 420 Inner City, and during 1820 both Mayrhofer and Senn, who were both Schelling disciples, found themselves being closely watched. Chancellor Metternich had a deep suspicion of intellectuals and found it useful to breed suspicion amongst their ranks. The dramatist Kotzebue was murdered by a student in March because it was suspected that he was an informer. This manifestation of resistance only resulted in even tighter police regulations and repression. Franz Grillparzer, the playwright was warned by the police after writing a poem that criticised the church authorities. Schubert himself was at a party in March in Johann Senn's rooms when the police raided and arrested Senn, Schubert and several others. Schubert was released but Senn was kept in prison for over a year and then banished from Vienna. In such an atmosphere, 1820 proved not a productive year for the composer, and he mainly immersed himself in writing his Mass and, without a hint to anyone, in the deeply moving cantata *Lazarus* which was to become another of his unfinished masterpieces.

Other acquaintances at the time were Anselm Hüttenbrenner, who had known Schubert since his school days, and his brother Josef who was a particular admirer and promoter of the composer. His opera *Die Zwillingsbrüder*, commissioned back in 1817, was now produced at the Kärntnerthor Theater. A rowdy element countered the friendly reception by those who enjoyed its light farcical qualities and Schubert, who was watching from the gods with Anselm Hüttenbrenner, refused to appear on the stage at the end. Vogl accepted the curtain calls for him. The reviews were generally favourable and Karl Unger wrote: 'Schubert has done himself credit with his first opera but is not yet approaching the summit of Parnassus.'

The turbulence of 1820 is reflected in the few compositions that he produced. Amongst the few were some key works like

Lazarus, and his continued attempts to match a poem by Goethe that strangely fascinated him, '*Gesang der Geister über den Wassern*', with the right atmospheric setting; an attempt which was not finalised until the following year. It is particularly reflected in the works that came to nothing, the opera *Sakuntala* and the Symphony in E the following year; and the uncompleted string quartet of December 1820 that ended up as the deeply promising *Quartettsatz* (D 703). In 1821 he was living alone for the first time, in lodgings not far from Mayrhofer's at 380 Inner City. There he tussled with the unforthcoming symphony but managed to write some of his most profound songs to words by Mayrhofer, Goethe and Schlegel. By then he had developed a closer connection with the Kärntnerthor Theater and may have thought his opportunity as an opera composer had really come. Early in 1821 the management had changed for the good, as far as Schubert was concerned, bringing in two personal admirers, Count Dietrichstein as Director and Ignaz von Mosel as Secretary. Both supported the notion that native opera ought to be supplanting the Italian invader and, with this encouragement, Schubert and Schober, on holiday in Ochsenberg in the autumn, started work on *Alfonso und Estrella*, a fine work musically if not ultimately blessed with the perfect libretto. At this time, too, he was given a paid job at the theatre as *répétiteur*, but his unpunctual habits and unco-operative ways put an end to this rather quickly.

At least he was becoming known and was in demand at the soirées of the well-to-do homes in Vienna. He attended reluctantly, for the sake of fees, but never fitted happily into such society. In his 1865 biography of Schubert, Kreissle von Hellborn was near enough to lasting memories to give an account of Schubert from this time forward that rings true and gives us a clear picture (here paraphrased) of his mixed character:

> Schubert was often drawn into musical circles in the society at Vienna. At one such gathering Lablache took the second bass part in *Der Gondelfahrer* and, at a soirée given by Franz

von Lascny, Hummel, to Schubert's great delight, extemporised on the song *Der blinde Knabe* just after Vogl had sung it to the assembled company. It frequently happened that whilst the performers were loaded with compliments, not a thought was given to the little man who sat at the piano accompanying his own songs with an earnestness and depth of expression that was lost on his audience. But Schubert was very shy and chary of talk. While sitting at the piano he would become very serious and as soon as his task was ended he would withdraw from the room. He seemed indifferent to praise and applause and indeed disliked people paying compliments. At one party at the house of Princess Kinsky, the hostess stepped forward, embarrassed that the performers had been praised but not the composer, and, excusing her guests, said a few kind words on his behalf. Schubert ungraciously muttered that she really need not bother as he much preferred to remain un-noticed. But it was very different when he escaped from these social events and was in the company of friends at a convivial party. Then he would become merry and jovial, talking happily, telling jokes and generally acting the fool. Schwind has told that one of his favourite party acts was a parody of the 'Erl-King' which he would perform on comb-and-paper. His mirth, it has been recalled, was expressed in a hoarse suppressed chuckle.

He never danced but would willingly extemporise dance music for hours on end at the piano, repeating the items that he liked so that he could fix them in his memory for later commitment to paper. He always showed a great respect for the music of others, even those of lesser stature than himself like Zumsteeg, whose *Lieder* he often praised, and Conradin Kreutzer. To those who said that his own works were far better he would reply that he much admired their professional skills and wished he could write like them.

His liking for the wine is well known, to the point of earning him a reputation as a confirmed drunkard. He liked wine of good quality and, contrary to the common Viennese custom, refused to dilute it with water. As he appeared not to have a particularly strong head for drink he frequently overshot the mark at parties and in wine cellars when a good vintage was available. Then he would become boisterous, even violent. Later, when completely fuddled, he would slink off to a corner and brood in silence. In this addiction he had much in common with Beethoven. Wilhelm Chézy said that, at these moments, Schubert sat in his corner and nursed himself into a passion, quietly destroying glasses, plates and cups, simpering and screwing his eyes up. On one occasion at a wine-shop he played a game at which his friends had to guess how many pints he had consumed. Schwind reckoned that Schubert seriously damaged his health by these excesses and it contributed to his early death. It was perhaps the cause of the pains and rushes of blood to the head from which he suffered and which helped him to succumb in the end to a not very serious illness. If he had to be watched when the wine was around, and occasionally kept out of brawls, particularly with incompetent musicians, he balanced his evening excess by starting work early in the morning, often while still in bed, and by working hard during the day. The solidity and number of his works bear witness to the proper use of his time. He usually kept away from the performances of his own works. After a day working in solitude he much preferred companionship and a convivial evening.

4 COMPOSER IN PRINT

By 1821 Schubert was hovering on the brink of becoming a success and he was offered plenty of help by his lawyer friend, Leopold von Sonnleithner, and others, such as Leopold's father and uncle, who founded the Vienna Philharmonic Society. At gatherings in the Sonnleithner household, Schubert's songs were regularly heard and, although few of them still got published, they were passed round in handwritten copies. An event in this respect was a public concert at the Kärntnerthor Theater on 7 March 1821 when Michael Vogl sang *Erlkönig* (written way back in 1815), accompanied by Anselm Hüttenbrenner. There was great applause and an encore was called for. But as yet no commercial publisher would consider this example of 'modern' song. So Leopold von Sonnleithner, Josef Hüttenbrenner and others got together and published it privately (printed by Diabelli) and did very well out of the enterprise. For weeks after the concert the music-lovers of Vienna were discussing and admiring this song and others of Schubert's that were heard. Not long afterwards several of them were published singly or in collections by Diabelli on a cautiously negotiated sale or return basis. But at last Schubert was in print. Following *Erlkönig* in April 1821 came *Gretchen am Spinnrade*, four Goethe songs, including *Heidenröslein*, three songs, including *Der Wanderer*, five Goethe songs, including *Rastlose Liebe*; three songs, including *Antigone und Oedip*; three songs, including *Der Tod und Das Mädchen*; four songs, including *Erlafsee*; (all these in 1821) together with thirty-six *Original Tänze* (waltzes) in two volumes. In 1822 there followed *Eight Variations on a French Song* (D 624) for Piano Duet; three Male-voice Quartets, including *Das Dorfchen;* three *Gesänge des Harfners* (Goethe); three songs, including *Der Alpenjäger*; and *Suleika I* and *Geheimes*.

Vienna seemed ready to accept Schubert now as its special home-produced composed and Schubert himself might have indulged in a little optimism. But he was ever his own worst enemy. The arrangement which Sonnleithner had painstakingly made with Diabelli retained the copyright of the works for Schubert with a percentage of the profits on the sales coming to him after the initial printing and publication costs had been met. The collections of songs earned Schubert around £200, which may not sound much now but was quite a handsome sum in his time. For the first time he knew what it was to earn regular money from his craft. With his establishment as a composer, however, Diabelli offered him a down payment for the copyright of his songs and Schubert, without mentioning it to Sonnleithner, agreed to this. He made later agreements elsewhere but he had lost a good source of income.

As Kreissle von Hellborn records, Schubert 'was somewhat indifferent to the charms of the fair sex' and he was not given to passionate attachments. He had his affairs and once entertained thoughts of marriage, but it is highly likely, considering the predominance of male friends, that he was inclined to bisexuality. However, sex did rear its head occasionally and one night, probably after some intake of wine, he was led astray by some of his convivial friends and taken to a brothel. There were plenty of them in restricted Vienna. It was typical of Schubert's luck that he, of all the party that night, managed to contract syphilis. It was a common disease of the day and his friends tended to find his plight slightly amusing. To Schubert, however, it was not only painfully embarrassing, but depressingly painful as well, as he underwent the unpleasant mercury treatment that was the only known control of venereal disease at the time. The cure not only killed the disease but tended to kill the patient as well. Schubert, with hereditary weakness of constitution, further harassed by drink, almost gave up the ghost as his condition deteriorated. He spent the early part of 1823 in hospital. Afterwards, unable to look after himself, he was taken in as guest at the Schober household at 1155 Inner City with occasional recuperative visits to the family school and home now situated in the suburb of Rossau. He kept his spirits intact by regular composing but suffered much from sickness and recurrent depression. Illness was hard to bear and it was at this time that he declared, 'there is no man in the whole world who is as wretched and unhappy as I'. It was a miserable period after the omens of success. A holiday in Steyr at the end of 1823 helped to put him back on his feet again.

Schubert's attempts to break into the operatic world had been completely disheartening. The attempted revival of German opera was not only taken out of Schubert's hands but out of those who were his allies as well. Italian management and Italian opera came in like a plague. A few native talents survived.

Weber's *Der Freischütz* was one pocket of resistance. But the Italian strain dominated and, when Rossini came to conduct his own operas, he was treated like a god. Many people considered that Austrian music had gone into an irreversible decline. The Kärntnerthor Theater turned down *Alfonso und Estrella* and there was no more success when Schubert tried to get it staged in Germany. Even his greatest ally, Michael Vogl, slipped quietly into retirement. The one-act *Die Verschworenen* was also rejected everywhere. Next he worked with Josef Kupelwieser, now Secretary of the Kärntnerthor, on *Fierrabras*. This too came to nothing after Kupelwieser, despairing of the new trends and the demands of the successful singers, resigned his job and went to earn a living in other fields. The only ray of hope was his incidental music to *Rosamunde*. Although the play achieved only two performances, Schubert's heavenly score made a considerable impression, as well it might, and began to achieve considerable popularity. 1823 had not been without a continued string of publications and *Die schöne Müllerin* was in print at the beginning of 1824, followed by the vocal numbers from *Rosamunde* and two-piano arrangements of its instrumental numbers.

If Schubert more or less relinquished his operatic ambitions, he was still a composer in full spate, now producing some of his greatest music and at least regularly published, even if it was only a meagre percentage of his total output. Yet even the happy social world of the Schubertians and the intellectual gatherings of which Schober was the centre were gradually disappearing. Some of Schubert's friends had left Vienna to find work elsewhere in less oppressive conditions. Spaun, Schober and Kupelwieser all went and the winter of 1823 saw one of the last gatherings with all these friends together. In the winter of 1823–4 he lodged with Josef Huber at 1187 Inner City. By 1824 even the Sonnleithner evenings were discontinued. Life now became lonelier, more inward looking, and moving toward some hinted tragedy. How Schubert must have remembered the happier days, particularly those when he and his friends travelled off by coach to Atzenbrugg, a country estate which Schober's uncle managed, scenes from which, of the journey and the games there, have been so vividly immortalised by Kupelwieser around 1820. It was there, too, in the summer evenings that Schubert jotted down some of those most revealing and poignant little dances for the piano that seem to be right at the heart of his creative imagination, and from which the magical essence of *Rosamunde* and the 'Unfinished' Symphony grew, a spirit that makes even his most sombre works glow a little with remembered happiness.

From the strange interlude of the 'Unfinished' saga we can follow the twists and turns of Schubert's mind through a series of strange moods, grasping at happiness at one moment, plunged into deep depression the next. It was a journey from the romantic and naive tragedy of *Die schöne Müllerin* to the despairing world of *Winterreise*.

With Spaun in Linz, Schober in the Breslau theatre, Kupelwieser in Rome and Senn banished, Schubert's natural need for friendship led him to new acquaintances. The talented young painter Moritz von Schwind became an intimate friend; and he worked and relaxed with Eduard von Bauernfeld, who had ambitions to write for the theatre. He kept in touch with old friends like Kupelwieser, to whom he wrote on 31 March 1824:

> Imagine someone whose health will never be right again, and whose sheer despair makes things ever worse rather than trying to improve matters; imagine someone whose highest hopes have been dashed and to whom the happiness of love and friendship bring only pain; whose enthusiasm for all things beautiful threatens to forsake him – and I ask you if such a one is not a wretched and unhappy being? Each evening when I retire to bed I hope I may not wake again; and each morning brings back yesterday's grief.

He goes on to say that the visits of Schwind at least kept him sane and that he had written two more operas for nothing. More promisingly, he told of two quartets and an octet which he had composed and how 'I intend to pave my way towards a grand symphony in that manner'.

But such letters need not be taken as literally true of his total existence. Bleak depression at nine o'clock can turn to optimism at eleven when the adrenalin is flowing and several pages have been written. Schubert's friends often wrote to one another with news of him. Schwind writing to Schober reported that he was well and 'inhumanly busy', working with great zest on that Octet (D 803) mentioned above, producing a sunny work, commissioned by an amateur clarinettist, Count Troyer, and modelled on Beethoven's Septet, thriftily using as the theme for a set of variations in one movement a light-hearted duet, of 'Trout'-like quality, from his opera *Die Freunde von Salamanka*. Schubert certainly knew the value of his own themes, for he similarly pillaged one of his 1817 songs, *Der Tod und das Mädchen*, as material for the D minor Quartet (D810). He had success at this time with the melodious vocal quartet *Der Gondelfahrer* and wrote many more of his enchanting waltzes. So all was not despair.

The summer of 1824 was spent at Zseliz Castle with the Esterházys; Schubert by now elevated from being one of the servants to a friend of the family. As before, the requirements of the period dictated his practical music-making and the main product of the working vacation was some excellent music for piano duet, the Grand Duo (D812), *Eight Variations on an Original Theme* (based on a spritely march tune) (D813), the *Divertissement à la Hongroise* (D818), and many dances. A degree of optimism returned. 'Times are bad,' he wrote. 'But I try to beautify grim reality with my imagination. I am more able now to find peace and happiness in myself.' At Zseliz he found his favourite pupil Karoline Esterházy now an attractive nineteen-year-old and he enjoyed a mild flirtation. In writing to Schwind to say that he missed him and other friends, he hinted: 'I long greatly for Vienna . . . in spite of the attractions of a certain star.'. He was in fluent mood and wrote a part-song, at the suggestion of the Countess, to a poem she liked, during the same day. In between he suffered his usual depressions and found the state of the world disagreeable.

He returned to the family home at Rossau in October and stayed there until February 1825, writing a few songs in between domestic commitments. Feeling the need for creative solitude, he moved to No. 100 in Wieden, a lodging next to the Karl Church, a few doors away from the Schwind family residence. It was a low, attractive house with a flower-bedecked courtyard (now 9 Technikerstrasse, Vienna IV) and there he stayed until summer 1826, on his own for the second time, but conveniently near friends and a ready free meal. The desire to write operas had been diminished by frustration and he even turned down a libretto offered to him by Seidl. His sights were now constantly set on the production of a 'grand symphony' – though his constant references to it in letters and elsewhere have only helped to deepen the mystery of which symphony he was actually referring to.

Throughout his career Schubert was a fervent admirer of Beethoven, the great contemporary lion of Viennese music whose life spanned his own. In his music he constantly battled against being too much influenced by Beethoven's great and powerful example so that he might create his own style. He was brought up on Beethoven and made every effort to hear every work of his performed in Vienna. He had been at the first night of the revised *Fidelio* in 1814 and in 1824 he had sat and listened to the great composer, now fifty-four and stone deaf, movingly conduct the first performance of the *Choral* symphony and his *Missa Solemnis.* If anything was likely to propel Schubert toward a great symphony it was this. There was twenty-seven years difference in their ages. Beethoven was a great celebrity when Schubert was still seen as a struggling amateur. Schubert must have gazed on those stern features many, many times in his life, not only at concerts but passing him in the street – for they only lived a few minutes from each other in what was then a modest town. They may even have sat in the same taverns. By the time Schubert had earned enough reputation to call himself a composer, Beethoven was deaf and hostile. Schubert, seeing him approach, would take cover and watch in awe-struck silence. He once summoned up courage to pay a visit but left the door-knocker unknocked and fled. Another time Beethoven was out or not receiving visitors. On his deathbed the great man read through some of Schubert's songs that had been put before him and remarked that there was a 'divine spark' there. Whether he knew anything more of Schubert's music can only be guessed. No hand of friendship came from the famous German to the struggling Austrian. The nearest Schubert got to him was at his funeral. And after his own death he was buried in the next grave.

In summer 1825 Schubert went on a tour of Upper Austria with Michael Vogl, a repeat of the happy holiday they had together some six years before. For five months they rambled and rested, and Schubert was back to reasonably good health and full of high spirits. He was pleased to find, as he wrote to his father, that his works were known wherever they went and they were invited to many musical evenings where Vogl sang and Schubert played. In Linz they visited the Spaun family, who found Schubert 'relaxed, bright, friendly and communicative' on the one hand, 'serious, profound, inspired and full of talk of poetry, music and life' on the other. It was noted that, while in Gmunden, Schubert started a symphony which he hoped to have performed in Vienna during the coming season. So long labelled the missing 'Gastein' symphony, it seems likely and accepted now that it was in fact the 'Great' C major Symphony which Deutsch tentatively dates 1828 and numbers D944. The friends started their holiday with a fortnight at Steyr, moving to Lake Traun and Gmunden for six weeks, then back to Linz and Steyr. In August they moved to the spa at Gastein with its famous waterfalls, high in the mountains, where Schubert continued and may have finished his 'great' symphony. They met the well-known poet Ladislaus Pyrker there and Schubert set two of his poems to music and wrote a piano sonata with a joyfully Schubertian rondo finale. He wrote high-spirited letters home and to his friends.

In October he was back in his rooms in Vienna and wrote a number of fine songs and partsongs, but seemed mainly to be dabbling, writing the not very distinctive *Deutsche Messe* during the winter months, which was not performed. Usually such works were written for a specific purpose. If he continually longed to be back in Vienna, when he was there the growing prosaicness of its life generally seemed to depress him and inspiration came back only when he made an escape to the country and the mountains. He tried to maintain a routine: working hard in the mornings from quite an early hour, taking a break for a walk after lunch, then working till night fell and the candles strained his eyes, when he went to a tavern or coffee-house to spend the evening in wine-aided conversation or, occasionally, at some musical gathering. There were various attempts by his friends to get him into some sinecure post. In the spring of 1826 he was pushed into an interview for the post of Assistant *Kapellmeister* of the Court Chapel where he had once been a scholar. But the job went to Josef Weigl and Schubert magnanimously approved of the appointment. He was considered, on Vogl's recommendation, as coach at the Kärntnerthor Theater and wrote a trial song for his audition. However, when the singer complained of some high notes and asked him to alter them, Schubert refused and walked out. A brief flirtation with opera came when Bauernfeld produced a libretto which was rejected by the censor. Schubert had got as far as a few sketches and there the project ground to a halt. He was well-known enough by now, at least in Vienna and the surrounding districts, but he was earning little and not making the advance that his friends would have liked to have seen. In June 1826 he took a brief holiday in nearby Wëhring with Schwind at the summer house of the Schober family, producing a String Quartet in G. After this he moved back to rooms with Schober at 765 Inner City for a few months. By Christmas he had rooms of his own again nearby.

In August even Schubert had begun to think he ought to be doing more about his future and, prompted by his friends, wrote to two Leipzig publishers, Breitkopf & Härtel, and Probst, asking if they would like to publish some of his works 'on reasonable terms' so that he might gain some outlet in Germany. Breitkopf & Härtel replied that, as Schubert was still a novice, they might publish some piano music if he would accept free copies in lieu of payment. Schubert did not pursue that one. Probst got as far as asking him to send some pieces but when he did began, likewise, to try to cut the fee; and that possibility also failed. Probst returned to producing a collected edition of Kalkbrenner's works. The symphony he had so enthusiastically produced at Gastein was considered rather too difficult for the Philharmonic Society to whom he offered it with the promises of a dedication. They thanked him for his offer and 'as a token of their obligation toward him and music previously played' sent a small financial token. The symphony was tactfully forgotten.

Schubert was no nearer to joining the musical establishment than he had been at the beginning of his career. Such worthy composers as inhabited the official positions, dull and transitory as their works were, managed to get their music played. So did the shallow hacks of the accepted opera circuit. Schubert remained not only a dilettante to them, but also a somewhat alarming experimenter. The cultural bureaucracy of the day saw no merit in encouraging an amateur with revolutionary associates and a head full of romantic notions. He had many private admirers and protagonists but the press had mainly slighting things to say. However, as the admirers themselves were now getting older, more occupied in their own businesses and married, even the encouragement that had come from the Schubertian evenings was now mainly a thing of the past. In March 1827 Schubert moved to a second-floor flat which he shared with Schober again at 556–7 Inner City in a house called 'The Blue Hedgehog'. He had a sitting-room, a bedroom and a small music-room at his disposal.

In the same month Beethoven died and Schubert acted as one of the pallbearers at his funeral. It was a solemn moment as they drank to his memory that night and perhaps some wondered if the small, befuddled genius in their midst could ever succeed the mighty departed master. In gloomiest mood again he darkly sat and wrote a fate-ridden cycle of songs called *Winterreise*. He promised his friends that they would be surprised when they heard them. And they were. The bitterness and sense of despair in them made even Schober quail, and nobody really felt that such depressive works could do much for the composer's future. Schubert thought them the best thing he had ever done, and posterity is inclined to agree with him. It was here that he took *Lieder* writing, in which he was ever a pioneering figure, to its greatest heights. Yet such individualism as they showed was the cause for his comparative failure. To some he may have seemed old-fashioned in his liking for established forms; to others he seemed over-daring in his harmonies. The works of Hummel, Ries and Kalkbrenner were written in answer to the fashionable demand of their time. Schubert's seemed strange and uncomfortable, and publishers issued them mainly through their reluctant sense of duty to music as an art.

Winterreise was published in January 1828. It represented one side of his character. The other, in some ways the real Schubert, at least the one given spirit by temporary happiness and fleeting optimism, came out in the spirited Piano Trio in B flat (D898). There is no record of him hearing it performed. It was not published until 1836, and the manuscript later disappeared. By now, too, his piano music was beginning to formulate itself into something really distinctive. The fine set of four Impromptus (known as Op. 90) (D899) were published in December 1827 and had a reasonable popularity. He wrote many superb songs and the lovely *Ständchen* for contralto solo and chorus for Josefine Fröhlich to sing at a party at Lang's house in Dobling. He dabbled, as Mozart did in his later days, with more of those fascinatingly sketchy and short dance pieces, and another fine Piano Trio in E flat (D929) was written in November 1827; and four more superb Impromptus (Op. 142) (D935) in December (but not published until 1838). In May and June he had holidayed in 'The Empress of Austria' inn in Dornbach. In September he visited Graz.

His final year, 1828, conformed to the now settled pattern of hope and despair. To some extent he seemed to have come to terms with his life and he produced some of his greatest and profoundest music, including the E flat Mass, the three *Klavierstücke*, the songs that were eventually published as *Schwanengesang* (some written much earlier) and, what many consider to be his supreme work, the deeply moving and integrated String Quintet in C (D956). The last Schubert work in the Deutsch catalogue proper is the strangely light-hearted *Der Hirt auf dem Felsen* for voice, piano and clarinet which was written for Frau Milder. She did not see it until September 1829 when Ferdinand Schubert sent her a copy.

Schott, the publishers, now wrote unexpectedly from Mainz offering to publish any works Schubert had to offer. He sent back a list with the E flat Piano Trio (already performed in December 1827, as he proudly claimed, by Schuppanzigh's Quartet at the Musikverein) mentioning briefly his operas and symphonies. The interest revived his spirits, and he set about putting some finishing touches and amendments to the C major Symphony and presented it to the Musikverein. They tried it, but the string players found it too difficult and refused to continue playing. Even at a concert after his death they preferred to play the simpler No. 6 in the same key.

His friend Spaun returned to Vienna and there was a flurry of music evenings once more. It looked, at last, as though matters might be improving. There was the supreme pleasure of a public concert of his works at the Musikverein on 26 March 1828, when the Piano Trio in E flat was once more played, together with the first movement of his Quartet in G. The only thing to mar this triumph was the fact that Paganini held his first concert in Vienna three days later and the papers were so full of this Italian 'comet from the musical heavens' that all mention of Schubert's concert was pushed out. Schubert himself went to hear Paganini and was fascinated by the beautiful singing quality of his playing.

In September 1828, after disappointment and frustration had again began to gain the upper hand, he began to feel less well and moved into a room in his brother Ferdinand's house, No. 694 in Wieden. The comfort of a little attention from Ferdinand and his family kept him in decent spirits and working hard at many worthwhile projects. He planned a holiday in the mountains but decided, in the end, that he could not afford it; and he did consider taking lessons with Simon Sechter so that he would be better fitted for any official posts that came along. He drank with his friends; counterbalancing this, on the advice of Dr Rinna, who had suggested the move to Ferdinand's house, with plenty of air and exercise to try to alleviate the frequent attacks of giddiness and rushes of blood to the head. He still paid the rent at his previous lodgings in preparation for his return. However, his sickness worsened so that he was now incapacitated. At the beginning of October with Ferdinand and two friends he made a five-day trip to Unter-Waltersdorf and Eisenstadt where he visited and brooded over the grave of Josef Haydn. He drank and ate in moderation but was generally in good spirits.

On 2 October he wrote from 'Neue Wieden, No. 694 at the "City of Donsperg", 2nd floor, right' to the somewhat indifferent H. A. Probst of Leipzig (who had paid him some £6 for his E flat Piano Trio) a slightly desperate note:

> I beg to inquire when the E-flat Trio will at last make its appearance? Is it that you don't yet know the opus number? It is Op. 100. I long for its appearance. I have composed, among other things, 3 sonatas for pianoforte solo, which I should like to dedicate to Hummel. I have also set several songs by Heine of Hamburg, which have pleased extraordinarily here, and finally written a quintet for 2 violins, 1 viola and 2 violoncellos. I have played the sonatas in several places with much applause, but the quintet will be tried over only in the near future. If any of these compositions would perhaps suit you, let me know. With much respect, I subscribe myself, Franz Schubert.

On his return to Vienna at the end of October his sickness increased. Dining at the 'Zum roten Kreuz' hotel in Himmelpfortgrund (a favourite haunt) one evening, he had hardly swallowed a mouthful of the fish course when he put down his knife and fork and said that the food tasted like poison to him. This distaste for food stayed with him and he took very little else but medicine from then on. He went for regular walks and, on the morning of 3 November, walked to Hernals to a performance of a requiem composed by Ferdinand. After the service he went for a long walk and returned to his flat feeling very tired. The next day he went with a piano-teaching friend, Wolfgang Josef Lanz, to call on Simon Sechter to arrange the lessons which would largely be a joint study of the theory of music. Hours were fixed for the weeks to come. He continued to work until 11 November, on which day he felt so weak and depressed through a continual lack of sleep that he stayed in bed. Dr Rinna called once or twice but fell ill himself and a Dr Behring took over. He reported the daily state of Schubert's health to Schober. Schubert tried hard to get well, taking his medicine regularly, keeping a watch hanging by his bed so that he would not miss any of the prescribed doses. He managed to get up a few times and spend a few hours correcting proofs of his *Winterreise*. On the 16th he suddenly deteriorated and the doctor diagnosed an attack of nervous fever. He was still expected to recover and his friends visited him regularly – Spaun, Bauernfeld, Josef Hüttenbrenner and Franz Lachner among them. Lachner told Kreissle:

> Schubert, when I saw him, was in full possession of his mental faculties and I talked with him for several hours. He told me of his plans for the future, looking forward to his recovery so that he could get on with the opera *Der Graf von Gleichen* which he and Bauernfeld had started writing. He had sketched out quite a considerable part of the opera.

On that day Schubert's father had written to Ferdinand asking him to pray for help and trust in the wisdom and goodness of God. He asked for Schubert to be given the holy sacraments but hoped that he would gain strength and survive. On the afternoon of Wednesday 19 November, at three o'clock, Schubert died with Ferdinand and the doctor at his side. His last words, as he looked fixedly into the doctor's eyes and grasped at the wall with his hand, were: 'Here is my end.'

His father put out an obituary notice, announcing that the funeral would be at the parish church of St Joseph in Margarethen on the 21st. Ferdinand, recalling that Schubert had said to him in his final delirium, not sure where he was: 'Beethoven does not lie here', was able to arrange that his body should be taken to the cemetery at Währing after the funeral and buried in a grave beside Beethoven's.

The family that survived Schubert, besides his father and stepmother, were his brothers Ferdinand, then a professor at St Anna; Ignaz, still teaching in his father's school at the Himmelpfortgrund; Carl the painter; and Thérèse (Schneider) who was married to a professor at the Imperial Institute for Orphans. There were four surviving children from his father's second marriage, Maria, Josefa, Andreas and Anton, whose ages ranged between fourteen and three.

His friends were heartbroken. Schwind, in Munich, wrote to Schober: 'I have wept for him as if he was my brother, but I am glad that he has died in his greatness and has come to the end of his sorrows. The more I realise his nature, the more I see what he suffered. The memory of him will always be with us and all the troubles of the world will not prevent us from a deep feeling for all that has vanished with him.' Bauernfeld wrote in his diary: 'Yesterday Schubert died. I spoke to him on Monday. On Tuesday he was delirious. On Wednesday he was dead. To the end he talked to me about our opera. It all seems like a dream.' Spaun wrote: 'Poor Schubert, so young and only at the beginning of a brilliant career! What a wealth of treasures his death has deprived us of.' On his grave an epitaph by Grillparzer was inscribed: 'The art of music here entombed a rich possession, but even far fairer hopes.'

The report on his death listed his final possessions as three cloth dress coats, three frock coats, ten pairs of trousers, nine waistcoats, one hat, five pairs of shoes, two pairs of boots, four shirts, nine neckerchiefs and pocket handkerchiefs, thirteen pairs of socks, one sheet, two blankets, one mattress, one featherbed cover and one counterpane. Apart from some old music besides, estimated at 10 fl., no other belongings of the composer were to be found. The final expenses of the illness and funeral, as reckoned by Ferdinand, were 325 fl. 46 kr. Ferdinand kept all the surviving manuscripts and later catalogued them before many were sold. By this time, Schubert manuscripts were scattered around and in many hands. Many must have disappeared for ever.

IV The Music

Our assessment of Schubert's music can only be as intuitive as his method of writing it. By most artistic standards, the textbook norms, he is a perplexing writer. To begin with, in spite of the enormous amount of research done by Otto Deutsch and others, we know very little about his method, his influences or his knowledge. Musicology is a study of the end product. It is 75 per cent assumption. Nobody really knows how the composer works or if he was even aware of the design found in the scholar's subsequent blueprint. Schubert has a number of perplexing and conflicting facets that have led commentators to reach extreme conclusions. There used to be a tendency to think of him as being untaught or, at best, self-taught, which is to some extent true, in that he soon outstripped the basic rules of music that were within the scope of those who taught him. But he certainly had a solid musical education from his family, various teachers and at the choir school he attended. He did not receive an academic 'conservatoire', university-level musical education in modern terms, but this was no hindrance. The realms of higher education are not meant for the likes of Schubert. More often than not, the musical academy stifles genius or simply leads it into competitive areas of cleverness and complexity. One imagines that Schubert had neither a liking nor a desire for such a viewpoint. He had his own thoughts to express and he would find the way of expressing them by choice and from the example of the music that he heard (and undoubtedly he was able to hear a lot in Vienna), not only hearing but also performing it. His musical education, like Mozart's, was an eminently practical one, but not too strictly directed. No great composer is taught his art anyway. If we must dismiss the suggestion that Schubert was a musical ignoramus (which the craft of his music does for us very adequately) there is no need to lean to the extremes of those earnest and well-meaning protagonists who want us to accept the view that Schubert (or any other composer, for that matter) had a perfectly clear and intellectual view of what he was doing. There is still an attractive suggestion of amateurishness about his whole working life. The word is not used to suggest any lack of technique or imagination; but simply a haphazard productivity. In only one field of writing, his songs, did Schubert ever show true directional development. Elsewhere there is little to compare with the logical exploration that produced the piano concertos of Mozart, the symphonies of Haydn or the operas of Donizetti. The 'unfinished' work occurs so often as to be almost a Schubert trademark. The ultimate truth about Schubert is simply that he was a lyricist and not a natural formalist. The lyricist aims for spontaneity, the natural intensity of the inspired moment. Such a spirit is hard to maintain in longer works. Mozart was also a lyricist but in a more diffuse way; for he was a master of cumulative creation. His ideas naturally shaped themselves into the larger patterns of the concerto and the symphony. Schubert's, generally, did not. Even his most profound and most successful extended works have, as a rule, an episodic nature. So we will consider him first as an orchestral writer.

1 ORCHESTRAL MUSIC

We can safely assume that Schubert learned his symphonic craft by copying Haydn, Mozart and Beethoven, and many lesser composers. Without direct evidence or his word for it, we might hazard a guess that he would have been particularly affected by such works as Mozart's A major (29th) symphony or Beethoven's Second. The latter, written in 1802 when Schubert was around five, must surely have been part of his formative education. Of all the works available at the time it is nearest to the Schubertian spirit. He wrote his own First Symphony (D82) in 1813 while he was still a pupil at the Konvikt, dedicating it to the headmaster Dr Franz Innocenz Lang as a sort of farewell offering to the source of his musical education which he was then about to leave. There is no doubt as to his acquired technical ability to write for an orchestra, while the frequent debt that the work owes to Mozart allows us to assume that its shape and texture, scored for a typical Mozartian orchestra, were of an imitative nature. The basic spirit is distilled from Mozart. We sense Schubert copying, yet already trying to escape from imitation. In the andante there is a haunting echo of Mozart's 'Prague' Symphony (No. 38) and the finale exhibits subconscious awareness of the 'Paris', (No 31). There are wind passages throughout that Mozart could have dictated from his anonymous grave. The composer's admiring leanings toward the cultured smoothness of Mozart are tempered by a youthful desire to produce something rather more modern. These touches he can only glean from the towering contemporary master Beethoven; so echoes of the *Prometheus* music and the master's piano sonatas help him strengthen his adolescent plot. Such suggestions do not belittle the achievement of a teenage symphony. As a challenge to the supremacy of Beethoven it was no doubt delightedly, if politely, received when first performed that autumn by the school orchestra. If the opening adagio and allegro vivace had a gentle hint of an *Eroica* boiling up, the ensuing andante leaned toward the divine slow movements that Haydn wrote in his later symphonies such as No. 102; the minuet and trio (a compulsory exercise then) are of a conventionality only enlivened by a hint of the Schubert-to-come in the trio, and the finale is really a very good attempt to write a rounding-off movement; a task over which even the mightiest of composers have frequently stumbled. It all availed little, for the symphony was not heard of again until 1880, when the first movement only was played at a concert as a curiosity. This first symphony, when played in modern times by someone like Beecham, who understood so well how to make such supremely unaffected and happy music sound meaningful, is a pleasant piece to hear, and certainly its andante deserves more than passing attention as the stirrings of a spirit to come.

Stylistic uncertainty on taking first steps into the symphonic world are understandable. By now the symphony had become the novel of musical literature; it was the accepted way to make a mark as a composer. A step which Schubert would have to take; unless he happened to be wandering by way of the opera stage which would, in fact, have been a more logical progress for his nature as a compulsive song-writer.

There is not a great deal attempted for orchestra before or adjacent to Symphony No. 1 but what there is offers an interesting contrast showing that, even if Schubert found the crutch of imitation necessary in moving toward the symphonic world, he was already in command of his own style in the briefer forms. The Overture for String Quintet (D8) written in 1811, although unambitious in phrasing, would be hard to place except as a Schubertian trifle. Of interest are the Minuet and Finale (D72) and *Eine kleine Trauermusik* (D79) written for wind instruments, the latter sometimes said (speculatively) to be written in memory of his mother who died in 1812, but probably intended for some more public occasion. It has that creeping melodic line that Schubert was often to employ (in the slow movement of the String Quintet, for example) and a very personal flavour. One can also turn to the sets of Minuets and Trios (D89) and German dances (D90), written soon after the symphony, (originally for string quartet but frequently heard in orchestral form) to find the potentiality of Schubert's own melodic ideas in simple but ingenious dances that might easily have been penned in the days of Lanner and Strauss, rather than looking back to the stylised minuet of Haydn and Mozart that Schubert employed in the symphony.

The Second Symphony (D125) of 1814–15, although generally seen as a twin of the First, being of the same scope and texture, already shows some remarkable steps forward into the imaginative future. Before writing this, and after leaving the school, Schubert had attempted an opera, *Des Teufels Lustschloss* (D84) which shows an awareness of *Don Giovanni*, *The Magic Flute* and *Fidelio*, and has a remarkable Berlioz-like overture; and had further flexed his orchestral muscles in the accompaniment to a Mass (D105) – conventional enough, but competent. The Second Symphony may have discoverable imitations of Mozart again (from the later Mozart symphonies such as the E flat (39th) especially) but the overall flavour of the symphony is never precisely Mozartian. It is of an earthier nature than anything Mozart ever produced. It is as if Schubert was leaning more toward Beethoven (the opening largo certainly suggests this) in an effort to escape from the Mozart-Haydn mode – while now clearly trying to find his own style. The shades of *Prometheus* are again present. The rather jovial andante, which you might loosely call Haydnesque, is almost true Schubert, a theme and variations that remind us of the later theme and variations (1824) in the Octet. The minuet is disappointing, a rough-hewn piece that lacks grace and wit, although the trio is contrastingly graceful. Even so, no true character emerges and one can only compare the movement unfavourably with what the earlier masters had achieved in this common form, however unfair this is to an apprentice symphony. The finale comes as a remarkable step forward toward Schubert's own individuality and the future in general. Closely related to the finale of the First Symphony the movement could be said, with hindsight, to look forward to Mendelssohn rather than back to Mozart. Certainly the Second Symphony can be looked upon as Schubert's major experimental work; a clear expansion of ideas and form, and a tentative feeler toward individualism.

Possibly Schubert felt he was being drawn too much toward Beethoven in the Second for the Third (D200), written soon after (late May to mid-June 1815) is clearly a lighter, slighter and less ambitious piece and yet, at last, here we are right away in the distinctive world of Schubert, heard in the charm and humour of the opening movement's 'allegro con brio'. The whole work has a nonchalant air that tends to disguise its concentration and drama. There are themes of a nature here that were to remain with Schubert throughout his career and are still to be found, not far removed, in the 'Great' C major Symphony. There is lovely writing for wind, with the clarinet especially favoured with thematic prominence. The allegretto might have been conceived by Haydn in his most happy frame of mind, especially the trio, but this is an unmistakable Schubert invention. It could be dismissed as fairly elementary writing by some standards, but it is too effective to be seen other than as a sample of guileless inspiration. By now Schubert is ready to present a Minuet and Trio on his own terms. This is no longer a bow to a conventional form but a move toward the exploitation of the native *Ländler* rather than the court minuet. So many composers often failed to produce a finale that lived up to the rest of their extended works that it is remarkable to find Schubert particularly strong in the finale of the Third; as good as anything Haydn achieved and it carries us right away from the eighteenth-century conventions to the world of Bizet. Though performed at a private occasion in Vienna, this delightful work unaccountably had to wait until 1881 for its first full professional performance.

The effort and point of producing lengthy orchestral works that had no tangible future kept Schubert working on songs for most of 1815 and it was not until April 1816 that he returned to the symphony to write No. 4 (D417). Lacking the perspective of posterity's hindsight, Schubert could not have realised the effective individuality of his Third Symphony and he clearly believed at this stage that something of sterner stuff was called for; so the spirit of Beethoven was once more invoked. The result is a curiously unsatisfying and slightly laboured work into which the true lyrical spirit of Schubert hardly enters, at least until the trio of the minuet movement. Schubert was attempting to act out a romantic role, as yet unpersuaded that he was not fitted for the part. The result was a work which is certainly polished and well proportioned but which has failed to catch the general imagination. It is like listening to a pastiche Beethoven symphony –

which is, however, a commendable thing to achieve at eighteen. Was he consciously aware of the mighty influence of Beethoven at this stage, while he made efforts to realise his own image? Later he added the portentous title of 'Tragic' to this work, a dramatic import that it never truly comes near to realising. In its finale Schubert always seems to be trying to escape back to the true path of the classical purity of spirit. In his diary of 13 June 1816 he recalls a fine, clear day in terms of the 'magic strains of Mozart's music' . . . 'O Mozart, immortal Mozart, how many, how infinitely many inspiring suggestions of a finer better life you left in our souls'.

The clean, clear opening of the Fifth Symphony (D485), written in autumn 1816, is a clear declaration of his intent to throw off the obtrusive weightiness of the Beethoven mode. This did not leave him as anything other than a deep admirer of Beethoven, but self-realisation came just in time to remind him that he was not of the same strain. In the light of a modern scholarship the Fifth Symphony may well seem like a step back into the world of Haydn and Mozart which, to some extent, it is. But not in any retrograde spirit or as a matter of failing to keep in step with progress. In this symphony at last, Schubert, though laying his foundations in the Mozartian idiom, achieves a work that is entirely personal. There is rarely any doubt that it is Schubert speaking. Here he has discovered the stable form that is to be the backbone of even his most ambitious and deep-searching works, like the C Major Quintet. The profundity of the Fifth is the ineffable profundity of Mozart; the tearful beauteousness of the perfect expression; often a far harder thing to achieve than the nebulous depths of thought hidden in a cloudy statement of romantic writing. Beethoven himself had already moved toward the same area in his Second Symphony, to which Schubert's Fifth is so closely related. And what a strange contrast to the Fourth, the would-be 'Tragic' which had everything except true individuality! The Fifth is a polished gem, its finale a finely balanced improvement on all that he has so far achieved. It was performed in the autumn of 1816 in a private house and then heard no more until 1873. What a blow to his spirit the neglect of such a radiant and right work must have been!

In the late autumn of 1816 Vienna began to be reinfused with a strong dose of Italian opera, notably in the shape of the ebullient and infectious music of Rossini. Some seven or eight of his operas were performed in Vienna between 1816 and 1820, including the immortal *Barber of Seville*. Beethoven was disgusted by the airy triviality of the music, though generous enough to admire its craftsmanship and melodiousness. Weber disliked it enough to become genuinely hostile. It was all understandable. Mozart had had the same trouble before. But Schubert was outside such partisan areas. He went, with the rest of Vienna, to hear the Rossini operas and, on the whole, found them vastly amusing though not beyond a little harmless fun-poking. He absorbed a little of the Italian idiom which was not far removed in any case from the alpine rooted folk music of Austria; and his own operas of the time inclined toward the Rossini mode. Schubert was ever a magpie by nature. The most direct evidence of his interest came in the two overtures 'in the Italian style' (D590) and (D591) which he wrote in 1817. The Italian element was parodied in the rollicking rhythms, emphasised by the basses, and the leaping melodies. What happened, and very much to the good, was that Schubert discovered a new folky freedom of idiom that mixed in very well with his own style and added a new dimension to it. The Italian overtures may not be rated very high in Schubert's output but they have considerable significance and cannot be ignored. The first overture in D introduces a very famous Schubertian tune – the largo that later found its true home in the *Rosamunde* music. It is an Italian-styled tune modelled to a Schubertian train of thought. The Overture in C is more directly modelled on Rossini but lacks Rossini's own gift for irresistible melody.

The joviality and rhythmic zest of the overtures clearly overflowed into the Sixth Symphony (D589) written between October 1817 and February 1818. It is a light-hearted, tuneful little work, though it has less poise, polish and overall strength than the Fifth Symphony. Its lack of purpose has given it less appeal in the concert hall, and it is typical of Schubert's aimless artistic nature that his Sixth should be of lesser stature than his Fifth. In its own right No. 6 is a pleasant enough expedition to the shores of Italy and it is full of portents of what Schubert might have achieved with the encouragement of performance and comment. Perhaps it is its total cheerfulness that has left contemporary and modern opinion bereft of anything much to say about it. After its initial performance at the beginning of 1818 there is no recorded observation. No wonder that Schubert withdrew into his shell a little more and left the symphonic scene for some time.

It is only in comparatively recent times that Schubert's symphonies have been seen as a whole, and played and recorded as a group, in the way that Beethoven's have been for so long. Indeed, we must still reach the conclusion that, in spite of the uncritical advocacy of many Schubert devotees in print, they are still a fairly unsatisfactory group of works with their ups and downs, changes of mood and style, and their varying degrees of effectiveness. Schubert's orchestral progress was perhaps simply hampered by the neglect of each work as it came along. Was the neglect deserved? Certainly not. Each of the symphonies has a worthwhile and attractive character. The wealth of themes and ideas alone makes them satisfying listening. That Schubert never entirely mastered the longer form can still be said without it being a derisory comment. And neither did he really show a particular flair for orchestration. The orchestration of the symphonies is sometimes not worthy of their fine content. His writing is often thick and unrelieved by instrumental colour. It is the reason for the comparative lack of successful recordings which so often seem to present a dull wodge of sound, until the complementary genius of a Beecham sorts out the warp and woof of its threads. Schubert's symphonies do not have the natural purity and life of, say, Haydn's, which are so perfectly balanced as entities and so effectively orchestrated that they are invariably successful in performance. It is impossible to avoid comparing

Schubert's symphonic output with that of Beethoven, in whose shadow he lived and whose ideas almost overwhelmed his own thinking. The nearness in time and the coincidence of numbers offer a contrast that is somewhat damaging to Schubert's reputation. Schubert's First and Second symphonies are trial pieces, pleasant enough but only surviving by a whisker: Beethoven's First, though a similar copy of Mozart, is a sturdy work in its own right, his Second is a divine masterpiece, a work of serenity and poise that has little debt to anything but Beethoven's own genius. Schubert's Third is a light-hearted gem: Beethoven's is a towering masterpiece, heroic in every way, with the kind of organic tune in its finale that Schubert must have thought magical and tried hard to emulate. Schubert's Fourth is sturdy but without distinctive character: Beethoven's is not his major effort but has impressive qualities. Schubert's Fifth is a poised gem: Beethoven's is a dramatic *tour de force*. Schubert's Sixth is a jolly trifle: Beethoven's is one of the most perfect and pellucid symphonies ever written. Beethoven moves into a profund mood in his Seventh: Schubert's .... well, what happened?

If Schubert's symphonic output was irregular and tentative up to this point, the final products have left the world in total and, even now, largely unsorted, confusion. Alfred Einstein, in his 1951 book on Schubert, optimistically took the opportunity 'to clear up once and for all the confusion surrounding the sequence and numbering of Schubert's symphonies'. Nos. 1–6 presented no problem. The correct sequence of the remaining four (he said) was as follows: No. 7 the E major Symphony (an unfinished sketch which Schubert started in August 1821); No. 8 the 'Unfinished'; No. 9 the 'Gmund-Gastein' Symphony (1825), 'the existence of which is now generally accepted'; and, finally, the 'Great' C major Symphony which has appeared from time to time as No. 10 but obstinately reverts to No. 9 in most people's reckoning at the moment. There is no doubt about the existence of the sketch for the E major Seventh (D729). Part of Schubert's long-standing plan to write a 'grand symphony', it obviously had pretensions beyond his ambitious capabilities.

The sketch, which occupies 167 pages, follows the general Schubertian pattern – an opening adagio followed by an allegro in E minor and E respectively; a second movement andante in A; a scherzo in C (with trio in A); and a final allegro in E. The introduction and part of the allegro were fully scored but after the 110th bar, the composer's dedication to the task seems to have deserted him. The whole idea was obviously there in his mind, for every bar of the work is drawn in; the tempos of each movement are fully indicated; the orchestration is indicated throughout; expression marks are frequent; even the word 'fine' is put at the end. There are indications throughout of what was intended and instrumental parts are partly written in numerous places.

In 1846 Schubert's brother Ferdinand gave the score to Mendelssohn, who never summoned up enough faith to complete the sketch; he may have intended to one day but did not survive to do so. Mendelssohn's surviving brother Paul passed it on to Sir George Grove from whence it became the proud possession of the Royal College of Music. It has been reported that both Sullivan and Brahms at one time considered completing the sketch but their nerve also apparently failed. The first completion was made by J. F. Barnett and was heard at the Crystal Palace in 1883, but only a piano score was published. In 1934 the conductor-composer Felix Weingartner reconstructed the score with a maximum degree of sense and sensibility, and left us a published version that at least fills the gap in Schubert's symphonic quest with reasonable taste. This version has been recorded. The symphony reveals some of the Italian influence of the Sixth but a nature that allies it to the Fourth. It is basically Schubertian but Schubert in an unresolved and indefinite mood. The scherzo is a compact movement, the finale is jovially Haydnesque. The outstanding movement, however, is the andante, a flowing cantabile theme in 6/8 which might so easily have been one of Schubert's masterpieces had he worked further on it. Weingartner orchestrated it beautifully, possibly better than Schubert would have done himself.

We have already delved into the history of the next, the

famous 'Unfinished' (D759) which Schubert began in October 1822. To anyone with an ear for Schubert's musical processes, it is evident that the opening of this symphony is a total manifestation of what Schubert's music aims at: a statement of direct beauty and questioning profundity. It is music that walks the tightrope of perfection. One wrong step and the act could end in disaster. In the first movement, 'allegro moderato', Schubert rides cock-a-hoop. The dramatically right reintroductions of the basic theme match Beethoven's artistry at its best. It is, in short, a sustained piece of musical inspiration and invention that Schubert never bettered. In most ways the 'andante con moto' matches this with a beauty of thought that leads to the highest expectations. To speak slightingly of this gem-like fragment is hardly to be thought of . . . but surely the faltering had begun. Isn't that phrase less angelic, and is it not brought back just a few times too often? This, if not handled perfectly, can be Beethovenesque repetition at its most irritating. In fact, the two movements, the whole of what we have complete of the 'Unfinished', are capable of perfection; but yet again Schubert is so demanding of his interpreters, so heavy with his orchestral colouring, that he makes the perfection difficult to achieve. The nine bars that we know of the proposed scherzo seem quite simply inferior. They in no way live up to what has gone before. In spite of convincing theories (and certainly the B minor section of the *Rosamunde* music could be the missing section of symphony) it still seems most likely that Schubert simply gave up – yet again. It is not (and has not been) beyond the bounds of uninformed speculation to assume that the pages of the symphonic score (which, in common only with No. 3, were loose and unbound, whereas all the other were in bound manuscript form) had been burned or simply lost by Hüttenbrenner. Two operas suffered this fate, as well as whole Piano Sonata in C minor and the manuscript of Mozart's *Ein Kleine Musikalischer Spass* which Schubert had given to Anselm. The ifs-and-buts remain and are the stuff of musical legend. It would almost be a shame if the matter was resolved.

So what about this lost 'Gastein' symphony of 1825? The theory that the Grand Duo for piano duet, written at that time, was in fact either a piano sketch or a piano reduction of the symphony is perfectly tenable, and Joachim's sensitive reconstruction of the symphony on this basis is a very convincing argument in favour of this belief. The idea, also supported by Schumann, that the Grand Duo was of too profound a nature to be simply intended for a piano duet, is tenable. However, Einstein's 'clearing up for once and for all' has been firmly contradicted by the collection of evidence and writings that make up a chapter in John Reed's *Schubert: the Final Years* (1972). His evidence simply points to the fact that the 'Gastein' Symphony was none other than the 'Great' C major Symphony itself. It was written in 1825 and simply revised at the later date of 1828 now usually attributed to it. Historians have chosen to ignore or overlook the writings of Schubert's acquaintances, such as Spaun, who said, in 1864, that in Gastein Schubert 'composed his greatest and most beautiful symphony'. Ferdinand also refers to it, saying: 'to the larger works of his last years belongs further a symphony written at Gastein in 1825 for which its author had a special liking'. The evidence accumulated, but remained confused by the Grove's firm assertion (having perhaps not absorbed these references) in regard to the missing 'Gastein' Symphony, that the C major (firmly dated on the manuscript as 1828) could not possibly be it. Ferdinand firmly catalogues the C major Symphony as No. 7 and it is thus that it confusingly appears in the Eulenberg miniature scores with the 'Unfinished', although properly dated, even more confusingly called No. 8, a viewpoint reflected in Hutchings' 1945 volume on Schubert in the *Master Musicans* series: a view still allowed to remain in the 1973 edition of the book. But perhaps we can finally put the confusion at rest by accepting that No. 7 is the very-unfinished E major; No. 8 is the semi-unfinished B minor; and No. 9 is the C major (dated 1825 rather than 1828) in spite of its firm entry thus in the mainly infallible Deutsch catalogue. If we would like to think that the ghost of Gastein has been once and for all exorcised, we could well be mistaken, though it is probably too late in history now for any more missing Schubert manuscripts to appear.

A view which Spaun expressed, that Schubert could never be made into a Mozart or Haydn as a composer of instrumental or church works ('whereas in song he is unsurpassed'), to which posterity has largely subscribed, and which still has some point, is not altogether obliterated by the rounding-off of his symphonic achievement with the fragmentary gem of the 'Unfinished' and the solid, profound and satisfying manifestation of the 'Great' C major (D944). Beyond doubt, there at last came a symphony from Schubert that measured up to the Beethoven standards. Its nature, in speculative hindsight, seems much more suited to the year 1825 than to 1828, where it would have been a bed-fellow of the C major Quintet. Even 1825 might seem too late a date, if we closely examine it after the romantic leanings of the B minor 'Unfinished', and if we had not already observed Schubert's strange advances and recessions in his other symphonies. The C major Symphony is very much a step back to the B flat No. 5 in style, outlook and classical form. Only its sheer scope and size, its 'heavenly lengths', which Schumann remarked upon in a totally uncritical frame of mind, give it that extra substance. At the time of discovering it Schumann also said: 'Deep down in this symphony there lies more than mere song, more than mere joy and sorrow, as already expressed in music in a hundred other instances; it transports us into a world where we cannot recall ever having been before.' The C major Symphony is, quite simply, the largest 'classical' symphony ever written. The theatrical spirit of Beethoven is thrown aside; the conceits of Mozart are abandoned; it is a direct Schubertian statement in the straightforward terms that he best employed. Beethoven's Ninth is a mountain, a rugged peak. Schubert's Ninth is a pyramid, a treacherous slope to climb, hiding all kinds of secrets in its impassive shape. It should correctly be regarded as one of Schubert's ultimate attainments; a point to which several earlier paths were leading him.

Schubert, we can perhaps maintain, was not a great symphonist. But he was an erratically interesting practitioner and his symphonies bring immense pleasure. Had they been orchestrated with the clear and imaginative touch of a Richard Strauss or a Mahler – what masterpieces they might have been.

2 THEATRE MUSIC

It is with no special logic that we turn next to the field where Schubert had the greatest failures in his lifetime and the least modern recognition, yet in a realm where his talents as a songwriter seemed to promise the greatest potential – namely in the theatre. Schubert himself devoted much time to writing opera and considered it an important part of his output. His failure to break into the theatrical world has been reflected in the almost total neglect of these works ever since and the almost apologetic approach to them in books about him. Their regular performance has been debarred (so we are told) by their inane and inappropriate libretti. But one would have thought that the interest of any music by Schubert would have been sufficient to have warranted performance and certainly on hearing them (only now something of a practical proposition through their appearance on record) the reasons for the neglect seem all the more puzzling. If Schubert was not a natural writer of large-scale works, the fragmentary nature of opera and his great gift for song made it an ideal sphere for his endeavours. The full appreciation of them is still to come and they deserve our full attention.

And, of course, opera was going on all around him, much of it very second-rate and short-lived, but with Mozart's *Die Zauberflöte* a shining example as a regular offering at the Theater an der Wien. Whether by 1811 he would have managed to hear much opera, except in the shape of the overtures that the school orchestra played, we cannot be sure. The pupils of the Konvikt were presumably allowed it as an occasional treat, as their mentor Salieri was very much an opera man. Anyway Schubert embarked on his first operatic attempt in 1811, his first attempt at a large work, not long after he had written his first known complete songs *Hagars Klage* (D5), *Eine Leichenphantasie* (D7), *Des Mädchens Klage* (D6) and *Der Vatermörder* (D10). His experimental steps took him almost towards completion of the first act before he discarded *Der Spiegelritter* (*The Knight of the Mirror*) (D11), significantly just before he was due to start private lessons with Salieri in the summer of 1812. To some extent it disproves a theory that Salieri led him towards opera, without depriving the old composer of the credit of offering future encouragement. Schubert had a strong interest in drama. It was already there in those early songs. The 'unfinished' tradition was also about to be established. He stopped work at the 206th bar of the seventh musical item, leaving his orchestration in sketch form only. It was indicative of the plague of magic operas and plays that *The Magic Flute* had helped to encourage (although it was by no means the first), that Schubert chose such a story, a magic play by August von Kotzebue, by nature an exaggerated parody of the type of thing that was then so popular in the opera-house. To some extent Schubert missed the point of the parody and cast his music in quite a serious vein. His apprentice orchestration, generally unsuitable and rather too thick for the voices, had not yet learned the proper economical approach to opera orchestration that Rossini could later have taught him. This was his first attempt and it was a craft in which he was a slow learner. He knew little of the possibilities of wind colouration or the need for a firm rhythmic basis to song. He wrote in vocal terms that would have been familiar to a choirboy rather than an opera singer and would have made impractical demands on his singers in matters of range and phrasing. It was a good seven-out-of-ten try, far better than might be expected of a composer of ordinary potential, good enough, certainly, to foster hopes of a future opera composer. Schubert had voluntarily demonstrated his interest but gave up when he tired of the effort. Lessons with Salieri that followed were to put him on correct, if old-fashioned, lines, with regard to vocal writing and operatic scoring.

From around 1813, while still at school, he became a regular theatre-goer and experienced many operas at first-hand. True, the opera-houses were mainly full of works by hack composers whose names do not mean very much today, but they should have offered some guidance. He would have heard Mozart and early Weber, and in 1804 he went to hear the revised version of *Fidelio*. Experience of Rossini, already discussed, came soon after. The end of 1813 found him at work on his first full-length opera *Des Teufels Lustschloss* (*The Devil's Pleasure Palace*) (D84) which he finished in May 1814. The text by August von Kotzebue had already been set by other composers so Schubert's efforts were probably imitative. Nevertheless its ambitious nature impressed the composer's teacher Salieri. It did not, however, achieve a production. Between September and October of the same year he produced a revised version with an enlarged overture. Around 1820 Schubert gave the second act of this musical white elephant to his friend Josef Hüttenbrenner as payment of a debt, and his servants used it in 1848 to light the fire. The plot has some resemblance to *The Magic Flute* (entailing some ordeals in 'the Devil's Pleasure Palace') and something taken from many more. The overture has a considerable impact and sense of drama; many of the songs have promising themes. Such a prolific young composer would not consider the neglect of his first finished opera particularly important and, in the following year, 1815, he wrote or started no less than seven operas.

There was *Adrast* (D137), which was intended as a full-length opera but ended up as one of many Schubertian fragments with thirteen numbers in various stages of completion. Then there was *Der vierjährige Posten* (*The Four-Year Posting*) (D190), a one-act *Singspiel* with libretto by Theodor Körner which is a delightful little work that deserves revival. Theodor Körner was something of a hero to Schubert. Hailing from Dresden, he made a great reputation on the strength of a competent drama, *Zriny*, set in the Turkish wars, and other successful stage works, including a number of *Singspiele*, the kind of ballad opera then much in vogue in Vienna. In 1813 Körner crowned his success by being appointed Vienna's Royal Court Poet and then ensured his immortality by enlisting as a lieutenant in Lutzow's Voluntary Rifle Corps and getting himself killed in August 1813 at the Battle of Gadesbuch, a few weeks before his twenty-second birthday. He had written a number of popular patriotic songs and greatly stirred the emotions of the teenage Schubert, who set a number of his verses to music in the next couple of years. One of Körner's successful *Singspiele* was an adaptation of a one-act farce, *La Vedette* (1812), which was presented under its later title at the Theater an der Wien in 1813 with music added by Karl Steinacker. It was probably a misguided effort on Schubert's part to decide to set, in enthusiastic hommage to Körner, something already produced, but he did so, writing his short score between 8 May and the 19th. It is frequently suggested that the libretti Schubert used were invariably inept and unstageable, but the circumstances do not bear that out here. The slight story is of a soldier left to guard a village and not relieved for four years. He marries and settles down, but then finds himself liable to be arrested, on his regiment's return, as a deserter. It is amusingly farcical and certainly no less believable or stageable than any number of opera libretti which have been produced that one could easily mention. Schubert, hoping to cash in on the *Singspiel* vogue, and hoping for musical success through the theatre, produced a sparkling and likeable score, probably better than many that occupied the Viennese stage at that time, at a period when he was certainly in full steam. He had written one of his most successful songs, *Gretchen am Spinnrade*, in October 1814, and *Erlkönig* was to come in the autumn of 1815. His fine third symphony was begun at the same time and the music of *Der vierjährige Posten* has great affinities with it. The overture is an impressive piece of symphonic pretensions. There are delightful, if not decisively memorable, melodies throughout, including an effective 'Soldiers' Chorus' (No. 6) and a romping finale in A that shows real operatic assurance. Whether Schubert's efforts were rejected or his promotional zest fell short, it failed to reach the stage. Johann Herbeck conducted a performance of the 'Soldiers' Chorus' in 1860, but the work was not fully produced on stage until 1896, in Dresden, with considerable amendment to the score by other hands. If the work is not a masterpiece, it is certainly of considerable standing and interest in the Schubert output, and has now been recorded by a distinguished cast.

Next came another one-act *Singspiel*, *Fernando* (D220), with libretto by Schubert's close boyhood friend, Albert Stadler. The story, described by the writer himself as a youthful infatuation with 'thunder and lightning, grief and tears' was destined to similar neglect with a mere performance of its final chorus, in testimony to its existence, under the conductorship of Ferdinand Schubert in 1830. The composer loyally noted himself in the manuscript as 'a pupil of Salieri'. After this Schubert turned to a weightier name and started to write a three-act *Singspiel* on Goethe's *Claudine von Villa Bella* (D239) in July 1815. Once again his judgment of opportunity seems awry, for the play, originally written in 1776, had already been set by at least seven other composers – though, to be honest, none of them had made much of a mark with it. The full score of the overture and Act One survive in the Gesellschaft der Musikfreunde library in Vienna with some fragments of Act Two. The rest is said to have perished in Hüttenbrenner's voracious fireplace. Sadly, of course, the opera shows tremendous promise in its lyrical sections, the parts where the natural song-genius of Schubert overcomes his often over-complicated and sometime unflowing scores. It could have been successful with more guidance. Lucinde's arietta, '*Hin und wieder fliegen die Pfeile*' and Claudine's arietta, '*Liebe schwärmt auf allen Wegen*', are of Mozartian elegance (both are included in a valuable recording of Schubert's operatic music by Elly Ameling and given earlier attention by Elisabeth Schumann) and they offer us a tantalising glimpse of the opera's potential merits. It got as far as a promised performance of the overture in 1818, which was cancelled, and finally first got on to the stage as a fragmentary curiosity in 1913. Hüttenbrenner started to make a piano arrangement of it but never finished his task. Piano arrangements of two numbers are to be found in the Peters Edition of the songs. But, once again, Schubert's ambitions were thwarted.

In November he started work on *Die Freunde von Salamanka* (*The friends from Salamanca*) to a text by the poet Mayrhofer – a two-act *Singspiel*. This was shortly after writing the B flat Mass which was performed in the Liechtentaler Kirche at the end of the year. The complete text by Mayrhofer has disappeared but Schubert's score is intact, together with the lyrics, and it can be judged as a well-balanced and not over-ambitious work that really ought to have been staged. It had a comic opera sort of story that no student of opera libretti could consider particularly outrageous. Lasting fame came to the attractive and memorable duet, '*Gelagert unter'm hellen Dach*', when Schubert reused its Papageno-like melody as the theme for a set of variations in the fourth movement of his Octet (D803) in 1824. Schubert's inspiration for this work might well have been his teacher Salieri.

By this time he was a fairly experienced composer with three symphonies behind him and the orchestral writing for *Die Freunde von Salamanka* is quite assured. The score is, for once, complete, a *Singspiel* that is well balanced musically and has most of the elements of being a successful operatic work. We cannot judge its total stage effect without the lost dialogue but here, it seems, might be the golden case for a revised version with a new and well-designed story, possibly with the addition of some other suitable material from less revivable operas. The lyrics are suited to their purpose and, on the whole, the work moves towards the realms of French comic opera.

At this point perhaps we can begin to surmise as to what Schubert's operatic aims really were. He had the Italian guidance of Salieri as a basis. He was a great admirer of Gluck whose *Iphigénie en Tauride* had so impressed itself upon him that, according to Spaun, he forthwith indulged in 'a most diligent study of all Gluck's scores'. The formalities of early *opera seria* and *buffa* were in process of being modified in the cause of the same romantic ideals that were motivating Schubert in song. The two forms were being united so that a serious opera could hold elements of humour and thence become more humanitarian and nearer to real life. In Schubert's time the *Singspiel*, with its spoken dialogue and deeper delineation of character, was the true German contribution to operatic development. Formality, a move which would be welcome to Schubert's ideals, had disappeared. It is said that Schubert was particularly influenced by *The Magic Flute* which, of course, had these elements – romantic music, the high aspirations of the *seria* branch with elevated choral writing in the manner of Handel, the sprinkling of humour in the shape of Papageno and the folk-like songs he was given to sing, slapstick, meaningful dialogue with a melodious score throughout. It was a supreme guide but hard to follow. But it had, on the grand scale, all the elements of *Singspiel* that it would have been natural for Schubert to develop: works full of infinite variety, a mixture of song and operatic aria, informal and formal passages, high tragedy and low comedy. Where opera had once been a sphere for classical mythology and Shakespearean tragedy, the age of Schubert was seeing its way towards cheerful stories about peasants and townspeople, poor as well as rich or, in less realistic vein, fairy-tales from the pantomime world.

If only Schubert had found a Chaucer to supply a libretto, his needs might well have been satisfied. He hoped that his literary friends, whose interests and inclinations were similar, would provide this kind of story in plain and simple language. Mayrhofer, Schober and Bauernfeld lacked, however, the necessary theatre experience and Bauernfeld admitted in 1869 that none of them had been able to supply the ideal text that Schubert longed for all his life. Schubert, for his part, appears to have thought deeply about these operatic ideals and tried to work them out with the help of Salieri and Ignaz von Mosel, the latter especially in sympathy with his ideal. But Schubert seems to have stayed in the same muddle as his librettists. Instead of writing his own natural style of music, he often moved back in time with his opera music, aping Gluck too much, and writing far too much in a choral vein with thick accompanying orchestral textures. Had he allowed the natural lyricism of his lighter songs and dances into these scores how much richer they would have become. With the example of Papageno before him, it is strange that he missed this point.

In 1816 he wrote two-thirds of *Die Bürgschaft* (The Surety) (D435), an elaborate three-act opera based on Schiller's ballad of the same name. The adaptor, probably one of Schubert's friends, preferred to remain anonymous, not surprisingly. Even Schubert, with his taste for tragic romanticism in literature, could not, in the words of A. Hyatt King, 'stomach the drivelling nonsense of the text' and gave up after completing the second act, with sixteen numbers completed. Individually some of these are quite delightful, particularly the romantic trio, '*Die Mutter sucht ihr liebes Kind*', and the quartet, '*Horch die Seufzer uns'rer Mutter*', both of which involve two children, sympathetically written for. But, on the whole, it simply meant a great deal more wasted effort.

Schubert then left opera alone for some time, possibly deterred at last by the fruitlessness of his endeavours, and the following year was mainly occupied in writing songs, part-songs and choral music. By 1817 he had come firmly under the influence of Rossini and had written some vocal pieces in imitation and the two Overtures 'in the Italian style' (D590 and D591). So he was well prepared for his next stage works which, happily and surprisingly, were the result of firm paid commissions. One of them came about through the influence of his friend, the well-known singer Michael Vogl, who was then a regular member of the Kärntnerthor Theater ensemble. The commission came from Georg von Hofmann, the secretary ('dramaturg') of the Kärntnerthor, who had adapted a French comedy *Les Deux Valentines* as a musical farce under the title of *Die Zwillingsbrüder* (*The Twin Brothers*) (D647). The dual role of the two brothers was a splendid chance for Vogl, and Hofmann, who was an experienced writer for the theatre, produced a neat and settable libretto, a story of mistaken identity in the W. S. Gilbert vein, nothing profound but certainly worthy of making the piece into a usuable curtain-raiser. As was Schubert's music. He seems to have started work on it at the end of 1818. The overture, probably written last, is dated 19 January 1819. After this rather Mozartian prelude, the work is cast in the popular *Singspiel* vein with easy melodies, and, at last, *Lieder*-like arias which remind us that it was written at the same period as the 'Trout' Quintet. There is a nice variety of harmonic and rhythmic interest. Karl Schumann, the annotator of the German recorded version, says:

> The melodic line in Leschen's aria 'Der Vater mag wohl Kind mich nennen' or in Friedrich's first aria (No. 6) reminds us slightly of the emotional world of the *Schöne Müllerin.* Franz's first song still follows in the steps of Gluck and Cherubini. The ensembles reveal a thorough study of Mozart's compositional style. The highly expressive introductory chorus in B flat major already displays the melancholy gracefulness of the music to *Rosamunde.*

In short, we find Schubert being very much himself and producing a neat little piece that should have indicated future operatic progress. Oddly enough, and perhaps characteristically, he seems to have thought little of the work himself. On the night of the first performance there was some barracking and Schubert allowed Vogl to take the curtain calls for him. It may have been partly another slight touch of frustration, for the promised opening night had to be delayed until 14 June 1820 (by which time he might have lost interest), as the theatre was busy presenting as many of the fashionable new Rossini operas as it could. In the end it was given seven performances at the Kärntnerthor; so it could be considered a minor success.

The other commission also came from Hofmann, who was the author of a piece written for the rival Theater an der Wien. Schubert was probably already engaged on this when *Die Zwillingsbrüder* came along and it probably attracted more of his attention. This was for incidental music for a magic play in three acts entitled *Die Zauberharfe* (*The Magic Harp*) (D644) – the popular magical theme again, a romantic piece foreshadowing *Rosamunde*. He was promised an honorarium of 500 florins for this work. The music hardly deserves the neglect that it has had. The piece was first performed at the Theater an der Wien on 19 August 1820 and had eight performances in all. Schubert did not even get his money. One piece, however, the Overture, was to have a continued history which we shall mention in a moment.

The next opera project was a three-act piece called *Sakuntala* (D701) with a libretto by Johann Philip Neumann, based on a play by the Sanskrit poet Kalidasa. It had some literary quality but little theatrical sense, being dramatically weak and immensely long. Schubert only fully completed the Finale to Act 1, in his familiar choral style, almost completed the Introduction and produced sketches for some eleven numbers. One of its bass arias was completed by Fuchs and added to a performance of *Die Zwillingsbrüder* in 1887. Otherwise *Sakuntala* sunk with very little trace. The Finale was published in 1829 but in 1885 Brahms advised a publisher not to revive the sketches. During 1821 the directors of the Kärntnerthor asked Schubert to supply two additional arias for Hérold's opera *La Clochette* (*Das Zauberglöckchen*) (D723). They were performed eight times but Schubert was given no credit, so his operatic cause was not helped at all. In later performances of the work in his lifetime his contributions were not always included.

In the autumn of 1821 he had gone on holiday to Ochsenberg with Franz von Schober and they began work on a three-act opera called *Alfonso und Estrella* (D731), not destined to be completed, however, until 27 February 1822. This labour of love shared by the two friends came to nothing. In 1825, Schubert still thought enough of it to send a copy to his acquaintance Anna Milder, then a successful singer, and asked her to help him to get a performance in Berlin. Her reply in March of that year expressed regret at finding the libretto entirely unsuited to the current tastes of her audiences who preferred tragic grand opera or French *opéra-comique*. In the circumstances she could see no hope for it. She would be delighted, however, if Schubert could write a piece individually suited to her talents; something new and in one act, perhaps an oriental subject with the soprano the chief character. The splendid Overture (which also has a further history) Schubert thought possibly too noisy and intended to replace it. Once again, in retrospect, and aided by an excellent modern recording, we may be moved to wonder how so much excellent music could be ignored. True, Schubert had retreated unwisely back to his Gluck vein, but there is much grace and beauty in the score. The action, however, is almost nonexistent and the long work moves slowly through its naïve story. The Overture was to get its due in connection with *Rosamunde*, but the opera was not performed, and even then a cut version, with Anton Rubinstein's *Festival Overture* used instead of Schubert's, under the direction of Franz Liszt at Weimar in 1854.

The music for the theatre produced in 1823 only deepens our wonder at its perfunctory neglect, for by then Schubert was producing fine scores. The 'Unfinished' Symphony had begun its strange career; the *Wanderer* Fantasia had been written. At the beginning of the year he arranged the overture to *Alfonso und Estrella* for piano duet, which was to be printed after it had acquired further fame in 1826. A one-act play, *Die Verschworenen* (D787) by Ignaz Castelli, had been published in a periodical, together with a modest suggestion by the author that it might make an ideal libretto in answer to the continual demand for such things. Schubert took up the challenge and composed the music, although he was becoming increasingly ill, during March and April 1823. The story, based on Aristophanes, now set in the period of the Crusades, was on the theme of striking wives. It anticipated Offenbach in having some fun at the expense of antiquity. Castelli's libretti indeed had possibilities, but initial approaches to the censor of the time, however, indicated that there would be difficulties there. For some obscure reason the title (translated as *The Conspirators*) was not liked and it was renamed *Der häusliche Krieg* (*Domestic Warfare*). If Castelli foreshadowed Offenbach dramatically, Schubert was well on his way to writing what was virtually an operetta and, as Karl

Schumann points out, indulged in 'the persiflaging of the "heroic opera" and the frivolant elegance of the arietta'. If Schubert did not remain as true to himself as he might, he certainly took some telling flavours from Mozart and some of the prevalent Italian composers, actually getting nearest to the operetta vein in the ariettas (Nos. 9 and 10 in the score). The finale fairly bounces along with Mozartian vigour. The whole score is full of delights and it is difficult to see why it (perhaps coupled with another of the one-act works) is not offered to the modern world more often, as Schubert's style is now so thoroughly appreciated. Schubert was not to enjoy the fruits of these worthy labours in his lifetime. There is said to have been a private performance in 1820, but the first public one was a concert version at the Musikvereinsaal in Vienna, under the direction of Johann Herbeck on 1 March 1861, followed by a stage production in August.

There were brief sketches for an opera *Rüdiger* (D791), to an anonymous libretto, made in May 1823. Schubert wrote his superb song-cycle *Die schöne Müllerin* between May and November, at the same time embarking on another opera *Fierrabras* (D796), based on an old French romance, the story an even earlier German legend, with new libretto by Josef Kupelwieser. If his *Lieder*-writing had by then produced one of his sustained masterpieces, the parallel opera activity produced a less happy work and miserable practical results. It was written in answer to a commission from the Theater an der Wien, and Schubert, anxious to please, composed the first two acts, some 600 pages, in ten days. He delivered his completed manuscript and the theatre management kept it for two years, at which stage the administration changed hands and the whole thing was shelved. Kupelwieser was actually paid for his part in the proceedings. Schubert never got a penny. Writing to Kupelwieer's brother, Schubert said: 'your brother's opera turns out to be impracticable and my music is wasted. . . . so I have composed two operas for no purpose at all.' In spite of which he seemed still determined and certain that the opera house would bring him fame and fortune; for he wrote to various friends and acquaintances asking for still more libretti. The overture to *Fierrabras* was actually performed in 1829 at the Musikverein but there was not a full stage performance until 1897 when Felix Mottl conducted it at Karlsruhe.

The most remarkable score for the stage that Schubert ever produced was *Rosamunde* (D797), consisting of nine superlative items as incidental music to a romantic play in four acts, *Rosamunde, Fürstin von Cypern* by Helmina von Chézy. The actual play, founded on a Spanish novel, is now lost and only the four song lyrics survive. The same nearly happened to Schubert's score but it was fortunately found in a cupboard in Vienna after an enthusiastic search for it by George Grove and Arthur Sullivan. It was still there, tied up in ribbon, untouched since its meagre two performances at the Theater an der Wien, which had commissioned the score. It was again Schubert's bad luck, so we assume, to attach his music to an unsuccessful play. The author was far more successful with her libretto for Weber's *Euryanthe*. *Rosamunde* was the kind of romantic nonsense, we can gather from press notices of the time, that the Viennese public of the day generally liked, but this attempt was apparently too much of a good thing. It was overlong and appeared confusing. Apart from the overtures and entr'actes, we have now no certain knowledge of where Schubert's ten items appeared in the text. Schubert is said to have written the score in five days and at least he had the satisfaction of seeing six items in print during his lifetime, although not in full score. That only came after the efforts of Grove which he recounts in an appendix to Kreissle's early biography and later in his *Dictionary of Music*. The overture has an even more confusing history. Lacking the time to write a new overture for *Rosamunde*, he took the original one from *Alfonso und Estrella* (the one he had thought too noisy at the time) thus making good use of an otherwise wasted piece. In fact, when the opera was first heard in 1854 somebody else's music was used in preference. The Overture in C that subsequently became attached to *Rosamunde*, and was published under this title, was the one originally written for *Die Zauberharfe* in 1820. It is a very attractive and now well-known piece in true Schubertian vein. Arranged for piano duet together with some other pieces from *Rosamunde*, it was published as Op. 26 around 1826–7, and thus became firmly known as the *Rosamunde* Overture. A charming piece of music in its own right, its most catchy melody had originally been heard as part of the Overture in the Italian style in D.

The music to *Rosamunde* (with its subsequent *Zauberharfe* overture) might be seen as the very core of Schubert's achievement and style. Vocally, coming after *Die schöne Müllerin*, its songs have the same quality in them; likewise the choral section which is allied to his part-song writing of the time – such as *Der Gondelfahrer*. The orchestral parts are in that melodious Schubertian vein, replete with natural lyricism, that had by now graced such works as the 'Unfinished' Symphony and the 'Trout' Quintet. If this was, to some extent, the Schubert of the derided *Lilac Time* ilk, it is nonetheless music entirely typical of him. Schubert's love of his folky tunes is shown in the reuse of the catchy overture melody on three occasions, while the B flat Entr'acte after Act 3 has the melody he used in an impromptu and as the basis of a movement of a string quartet. It also has many echoes elsewhere. The final ballet music tune haunts the *Moments musicaux* and flitted throughout his works. The plot thickens if we pursue the perfectly acceptable theory that Schubert, under pressure and short of time, needing a substantial piece of music as Entr'acte to *Rosamunde*, removed a final movement intended for the 'Unfinished' Symphony and used it for the B minor Entr'acte. Certainly there is something in the argument that this substantial piece is of a stature and style that puts it in a different category from the rest of the *Rosamunde* music. However, this is still an unproven theory.

It is strange that, after only two performances at the Theater an der Wien, the *Rosamunde* music should have attained such instant popularity. The vocal sections were published in 1824; the Overture and other items as piano duets in 1826–7; the 'Chorus of Spirits', a sublimely ethereal piece with wind accompaniment, in 1828. And since Schubert's day the work has become one of the world's favourites. It certainly helped to make him a widely known composer in those last years of his life; not as widely known or as published at he might have been, but at least a figure of some reckoning.

For several years after *Fierrabras* Schubert admitted defeat as far as opera was concerned and, perhaps fortunately, no more librettos were forthcoming from his friend to tempt him. The opera dream still haunted him and, even when he was struggling through his final illness, he was talking, in lucid moments, of a great new opera that he was going to compose. He discussed it eagerly with Eduard von Bauernfeld and described the rich orchestration he intended. Bauernfeld's libretto to *Der Graf von Gleichen* (which quoted a poem by Goethe) was not approved by the censor when submitted in October 1826. Later much of it was lost. Schubert's contribution (D918) was an introductory chorus dated 19 June 1827 (published later in 1868 in a revision by Herbeck) and eighty-eight manuscript pages of sketches.

In Schubert's time an opera was rarely staged for more than a few days. The runs of those that Schubert had performed were therefore not abnormal. Even *Fidelio*, now considered a masterpiece, had only three initial performances and two in its subsequent version. *Euryanthe* ran for some twenty performances but to lessening houses after its first week. Rossini's operas came and went. There were few that notched up respectable runs by modern standards, and only one or two with exceptional appeal such as *The Magic Flute*, the archetypal magic opera with the advantage of its additional and probably very significant masonic appeal, which had over two hundred performances, but even these were spread over a period of nearly ten years. As for those that did not get on the stage, bad libretti seem to be almost universally blamed. Yet anyone who has struggled through a volume of opera synopses will hardly see improbability of story or the ludicrous nature of the language as a barrier to operatic success. It is very near the norm that they should be so. One suspects, certainly after sampling the delights of the music that was to be heard in them, that there was something more to it than this. Even in those days, perhaps especially in those days, you had to be well and truly 'in' to get things accepted and staged or published. Schubert, in this aspect, was his own worst advocate. He neither pushed nor pulled his way to success. Many of his chances he spoiled by somewhat boorish behaviour. We might even go farther and, rather than denigrate his operas (as has become the custom) question whether they were not too good, too 'classy', for the general theatrical taste of the times. One has only to look at the list of productions at an establishment like the Theater an der Wien to wonder what was in all those unknown pieces, why they disappeared and how they ever got there in the first place. Take a significant year like 1820, when *Die Zauberharfe* was given its eight performances. The longest runs that year were accorded to a piece called *Oberon* with music by Seyfried (thirty-six performances); a play *Der Bar und der Bassa* (thirty); *Die Falsche Primadonna* – music by Schuster (twenty-eight); *Bettina* – music by Schuster (twenty-four); *Die Wildschützen* – music by Riotte (twenty). Out of the total of sixty-seven productions mounted, another eight had between ten and nineteen performances, including Rossini's *La Cenerentola* (eighteen) and *Die Müllerin* by Paisiello. The rest seem to average one, two or three showings. Most of the works are by names that would be wholly unknown to the average music-lover today, with only Meyerbeer, Rossini, Paer and Schubert seeming at all familiar; and they appear rarely. The predominant names of Schuster, Müller and so on do not mean much today. The suggestion is a theatre of mediocrity, perhaps dictated by its audience's taste, in which works of the quality and individuality of Schubert's would not easily find a place. What is less forgivable is their later continued neglect. With modern texts (for the old ones are not sacrosanct) a whole corpus of likeable music by Schubert could become more widely known; and, surely, will be.

3 CHORAL MUSIC AND PART-SONGS

Closely related to Schubert's operatic output, and falling somewhere between it and his major work as a songwriter, comes Schubert's writing for grouped voices in various forms. It is interesting to note at what varied layers of vocal/musical integration he worked in his different areas of writing for the voice. In the songs he tried for, and nearly always achieved, what A. E. F. Dickinson has called 'a phenomenal fusion of material', in which words were illuminated rather than underlined. His attention to the conventions of opera as laid down by his predecessors seemed to prevent him from achieving quite the same fusion there. On the occasions when he did, as in the occasional song-like episode, he produced his most effective operatic material. But in his masses and part-songs he generally (but with exceptions) tended to let the music dominate and the words to remain functional. In general it might be said that Schubert, although educated in every way under the wing and surveillance of the Catholic Church did not have a deeply religious (in the ecclesiastical sense) side to his nature. His few writings reveal a natural belief and trust in God and nature, but his thoughts, as demonstrated in his vast output of song, were almost predominantly secular and literary. He mainly wrote church music as a duty and an exercise, and revealed little of the religious fervour and glow of Bach or Handel. We might at least have expected that his melodic genius would have led him to produce another *Messiah.* We do not remember Schubert by any really distinctive section of choral music. There is not even an *Ave Verum corpus.* The edge that the Catholic-Masonic conflict gave to Mozart's religious music is lacking. Even his nature-loving friendship with God did not lead him to the exultant open-air quality that makes Haydn's *The Seasons* and *The Creation* so refreshingly muscular. Even in his choirboy days Schubert seems to have been thinking more of his secular musical activities. Four of his six masses are, in fact, early student works written for fellow sufferers. We imagine that Schubert was not entirely happy under the oppressive regime of a choir-school, and it was less a matter of religious fervour than religious duty that led him to write church music at all.

So no Schubert mass is a step forward in choral writing, nor particularly personable, nor tackled with the inner glow of conviction that we find in Beethoven's highly charged writings in this field. He writes his choral music in conventional block harmony form, with few notable solo excursions, probably modelling most of it on the works of the lesser Viennese church composers, who taught and surrounded him, rather than seeking a higher plane of expression. One feels that the formal words of the Catholic mass did not particularly move him. The pious formulas were simply repeated in formulated music. What musical experiment he embarks on reminds us simply of the way he exploited key relationships in his orchestral works and especially in the underrated but highly significant sets of dances for the piano. In the A flat Mass (No. 5), for example, he moves through the keys of A flat, E, C, F (and F minor) and back to the original key. But this is neither unique nor exceptional in such writing. He stuck to fairly conventional and accepted routines. The best study of these works is still that by A. E. F. Dickinson in the *Schubert Symposium*, edited by Gerald Abraham, which offers a detailed examination of each work; but ultimately arrives at the conclusion that none of the masses are particularly remarkable. In a popular survey, *Choral Music* (Penguin Books, 1963), Schubert is given little more than one page out of 444.

Schubert tried his hand at various Kyries (D31, D66) Cantatas (D80) and Offertories (D85) before first attempting a full-length Mass in F (D105) in July 1814. This was written for his local church at Liechtenthal to celebrate its centenary. It was conducted by the youthful composer, performed by a large orchestra with oboes, clarinets, bassoons and two horns, and made quite an impression on those who heard it, including Salieri. They were perhaps pleased to find it surmounting the conventions in an equable way, but there is nothing particularly remarkable about the music except for a few brief moments in the *Gloria* and the *Sanctus*. Generally the voices seem to be written for as instruments rather than as vehicles of articulate vocal expression.

The year 1815 produced two further masses; No. 2 in G (D167) which has become fairly standard fare, strangely, in the Anglican church, is again a fairly unremarkable work, curiously objective. Schubert makes the Kyrie a pleasant minuet with the slightly quirkish modulations of his dances. Because of the ease of performance it works well enough in practice and leaves a likeable, if short-lived, impression. The B flat Mass No. 3 (D324) came at the end of 1815, after writing such works as the Third Symphony, *Heidenröslein* and several operas, so it is not surprising that it begins to show rather more individual treatment of its text. If its overall spirit is complacent goodwill, every now and then, as in the 'Dona nobis pacem' of the *Agnus Dei*, one finds words heightened and some refinement in the general writing. It was performed in the church at Liechtenthal and was heard elsewhere during Schubert's lifetime.

The C major Mass No. 4 of 1816 (D452) was written while Schubert was teaching at his father's school and, again, was probably performed in the local church. It was used more than once during Schubert's life, almost certainly again in 1825 and 1828 when he wrote a new *Benedictus* (D961), published as Op. 48 in 1825 by Diabelli and dedicated by Schubert to his old friend and choirmaster of Liechtenthal, Michael Holzer, who had taught him the rudiments of church music. At this stage woodwind and timpani were added. Here Schubert draws nearer to the spirit of the *Missa Brevis* as written by Mozart. It is a direct and simple work with no greatly imaginative writing but we can enjoy the quiet touch of the *Kyrie* as it opens, the tranquillity of the *Benedictus* and some subtle writing for violins in the *Agnus Dei*.

Schubert embarked on several choral fragments during the ensuing years but made his next incursion into the full-length mass in November 1819 although this, the Mass in A flat (D678), was not actually finished until September 1822, around the time of the 'Unfinished' Symphony. It was first performed in the Alt-Lerchenfelder Kirche in Vienna. He wrote to his friend Spaun in 1822: 'My Mass is finished and will soon be performed. I still have the old idea of dedicating it to the Emperor or Empress, as I think it is a success.' He was discouraged in this bold enterprise by the Court Kapellmeister, Joseph Eybler, who thought that the mass was good 'but not composed in the style which the Emperor likes'. Schubert took the rebuff good-naturedly and was rather amused at the suggestion that he could not write in the imperial manner – which presumably, as has ever been the taste of royalty, meant something simple, tuneful and not too long. Schubert had taken this mass very seriously, and it was a long, ambitious work requiring large vocal and orchestral forces. He tinkered with it again, later altering the *Cum sancto spirito* and *Osanna* sections. The *Kyrie* is extended to five parts while the *Gloria* aspires to higher levels than ever before, reminding us that Beethoven's Mass in D (which Schubert may not have heard) was being written at the same time. Yet on the whole there are still no deeply heartfelt moments arising from Schubert's religious writing. It has to be remarked (and has been) that it is curious that he spent time in revising some of this work while he left the 'Unfinished' in such an unresolved state. Perhaps Schubert saw the church rites, and the mass in particular, in the light of a balm, a calming of the mind, a cleansing of the worldly troubles, a preparation for equable thoughts of God.

The final Mass No. 6 in E flat (D950) came in Schubert's last year just after the C major Symphony. As might be expected, it assumes a deeper nature than any of the preceding works, less formal, more developed. The *Agnus Dei*, moving into G minor, has a dramatic urgency not felt before. The *Miserere* is an effective unison figure. While not a revealing work, it makes an impression which much of his church music had hitherto failed to do. 'Worthy to be spoken of in the same breath as Bach's B minor or Beethoven's in D', says one faithfully enthusiastic protagonist; but we may not care to go that far.

The same uncommitted elegance that we have discerned so far is to be found in other choral works throughout Schubert's life. There is one work, however, that has some fascinating glimpses of the real Schubert escaping from its religious background, showing him applying the dramatic techniques of his secular literary writing to such a subject. Strangely, it is another of these ruin-like fragments that stand out in the Schubertian landscape – namely the Easter Cantata *Lazarus* (or *Die Feier der Auferstehung*) (D689) which Schubert worked on during the early part of 1820. The first act was completed (and dated February 1820); the manuscript is kept in the National bibliothek, Vienna. It was performed on 11 April 1830 (Easter Sunday evening) at Vienna's Anna-Kirche, probably conducted by Ferdinand Schubert, who then sold the one-act score to the publishers Diabelli. When he listed Schubert's works in 1839 Ferdinand still assumed that this was the only portion that Schubert had written, by which time it had still not been published. Then, in 1859, Schubert's first biographer Kreissle von Hellborn discovered the manuscript score of an incomplete second act in the papers of the Beethoven scholar A. W. Thayer, the score ending in the middle of an aria for Martha. Schubert indicated his intention of writing the third act, but if it ever got on to paper in any shape, it has never been discovered. The work was next performed, the two acts and the preceding recitative, at the Redoutensaal in Vienna on 27 March 1863 under Johann Herbeck who later published a piano score of the existing portions.

Schubert used a text by the then young Lutheran church councillor, August Hermann Niemeyer (1754–1828), which he had published in Leipzig in 1778. The text was previously set as a religious drama by Johann Heinrich Rolle but it proved unsuited to the stage and was heard of no more. Niemeyer slightly amended his text in 1814 and Schubert used this version with very little further alteration. The three sections were Death, Burial and Resurrection. Schubert's version was perhaps never intended to be acted, particularly after his other operatic ventures, nor would it have been likely, as Niemeyer was well out of favour with the Imperial and Prussian authorities and the police. A stage performance was tried at the Vienna Konzerthaus in 1928 but most resurrections since have treated it as a concert work. In spite of such promotion by Hermann Scherchen and others, and two German recordings, the work seems to puzzle and even antagonise most writers on Schubert. The scholars have not been able to settle the matter of its intended or actual completion, and there is no contemporary comment or any word on the subject from Schubert himself. This is more surprising than it might seem at first for 1820, when he was in poor health, was one of Schubert's least productive years, with only his finest A flat Mass being fitfully written and otherwise mainly a few vocal works and the unfinished opera *Sakuntala*. The score suggests that, in contrast to most of the masses, he might have spent quite a considerable time on *Lazarus*.

The mystical opening has none of the formality of the masses and the vocal line is far nearer to that of the *Lieder*. Throughout, Schubert adds impressively effective music to the difficult text and, as Bernhard Paumgartner has written, 'injects life into the recitatives and weaves a bewitching instrumental texture around the lovely arias and choruses'. It includes some of his best and most delicate accompanying orchestral writing, and he went further, in dramatic terms, than he dared in most of his operas. Alfred Einstein was one enthusiastic admirer and declared that *Lazarus* (seen in historical perspective) towered musically above *Tannhäuser* and *Lohengrin*. We need not let partisanship lead us so far. The fragmentary second act is no less profound and moving than the originally heard first act. Einstein particularly praises the depiction that Jairus's daughter gives of her death, the glimpse of Paradise and the return to earth. In the second act the chorus of friends is sublime in its tenderness. In many ways it is the most forward-looking piece of music that Schubert ever wrote. It is likely that, as with the 'Unfinished' Symphony, he found himself moving ahead of his time and his own still growing capabilities, and was unable to continue, as he would have wished, to improve dramatically on what he had already written. It remains yet another of those profound and enigmatic fragments that only add to our difficulties in assessing this remarkable composer.

In assessing Schubert's considerable output of part-songs and miscellaneous pieces for voices, we move immediately from his cautious religious output to a mainly secular world where he is more relaxed and often in his most openly melodic vein. Moreover he uses advantageously the less demanding textural weights to produce many works whose simple delights were intended for amateur performance and the pleasurable evenings that he spent round the piano with his intimate friends. A number of recordings have acquainted us with the best of these pieces, in the forefront of which come such items as *Der Gondelfahrer* of 1824 (D809). If only Schubert had placed more things like this in an operatic context; the contented song of the gondoliers over barcarolle rhythm, and the tolling of St Mark's bell as the harmony changes momentarily from C to A flat. The lovely *Ständchen*, (D921) of 1827, was written to words by Grillparzer for the birthday of Louise Gosmar, at the request of Anna Fröhlich with a leading contralto part for her sister Josefine and a chorus for ladies to sing. There were two versions: D920 which Schubert wrote by mistake for male quartet, and D921 which he rewrote the next day, as originally requested, for female voices. Many such works were rewardingly performed as soon as they were written and thus gave Schubert much of the limited pleasure he was able to gain from his own music; although often, as in this case, he did not even bother to attend the occasion.

If some of the best gems in this form came in his mature years, Schubert had been writing such music amongst his solo songs from his earliest days, some 135 such compositions in all. Walther Dürr, writing about these part-songs, puts them into an interesting historical context in a booklet accompanying a recent comprehensive set of recordings. I can only paraphrase, with apologies and acknowledgements, what Dürr so wisely says. Reminding us of the important place in history we accord Schubert's

Lieder, he suggests that the part-songs may well have a place of (almost) equal significance. They were almost inevitably written, as the songs were, in response to a need and stimulus; in this case two needs. The first was the growing demands of the rise of secular choral-singing societies, an art that was strangely absent then, with most of it done by official and religious choirs from schools such as Schubert himself trained in. Hans Georg Nagel wrote, in the midst of the Napoleonic assaults of 1809: 'The age of music will only begin when it is not only experts who devote themselves to the fine arts, but when the higher arts become the common property of the country's people ... This will only be possible through choral singing.' In fact, in those times, choral singing was generally in a poor way and it was only by composers and writers providing the right material that it could be revived. This was one challenge that Schubert answered well. A group called the Singakademie had pioneered this tradition under K. F. C. Fasch. A similar Singinstitut was founded in Zurich in 1802, and in Vienna in 1812 the society that eventually became the 'Gesellschaft der Musikfreunde' was founded. Anna Fröhlich, who became a close friend of Schubert's, formed a female choir from her pupils and Schubert wrote many songs for them, including the famous *Ständchen* (D920), mentioned above. So Schubert took an active part in the birth of a choral tradition from around 1810 onwards when he first copied down some of the part-songs of Michael Haydn and started to learn the trade.

That was one side of the story. The other was the strengthening of the long tradition of bourgeois home music-making that the Biedermeier period saw as the result of the oppressive rule of both the Austrian politicals and the invading Napoleon. Culture blossomed in the drawing-room, including those drawing-rooms where the Schubertians flourished with the good fortune of having Schubert, the most prolific source of such music, among them. These activities overlapped those of the choral-singing societies as these kindred souls were also amongst those who began such groups as the Gesellschaft der Musikfreunde. In contrast to his unadventurous church-music writing, Schubert experimented freely in the part-song field and achieved some real masterpieces, notably, for example, in his settings of Goethe's *Gesang der Geister über den Wassern* ('Song of the spirits over the waters'). This was a poem which seemed to exert a powerful influence over him for he first made a fragmentary attempt to set it as a solo song in 1816 (D484), followed by a version for unaccompanied male quartet in 1817 (D538) done in a polyphonic style that owed much to the old madrigal tradition. His experimental spirit finally led to a setting for eight male voices (four tenors and four basses) and five string instruments (D 714), in 1820; and even this had already been preceded by an earlier, discarded octet version (D704) and a four-part plus piano version (D705) a few months previously in 1820. All this indicates that much thought had gone into the final piece (D714) that was sung at a public concert in the Kärntnerthor Theater early in 1821. The now popular *Erlkönig* was performed at the same concert and won unstinted praise. The eight-part *Gesang*, however (as harmonious and noble a piece as you could wish, to our modern ears), struck the critic of the *Wiener Allgemeine Musikalische Zeitung*, speaking on behalf of his bemused readers, as being full of strange musical modulations and evasions with no sense, order or objective, the composer going along like a coachman with eight horses which he never managed to keep on the road. It does help us to put the elusive music of our own contemporaries into perspective.

4 PIANO MUSIC

Schubert himself made no comments about the piano as a medium and remarks regarding his accomplishment as a pianist are generally confined to the simple facts as to where he played it rather than how. The impressions of him providing dance music for his friends suggest an adequate and natural capacity at the instrument rather than any virtuoso standards. Schubert's other capacities stem from the accepted premise that he was most naturally and successful a songwriter. His desire to write opera was an extension of his dramatic appreciation which he exploited in his *Lieder*. His liking for and the depth of his searchings in chamber-music led him to make his most profound music in that form. He was not a natural orchestral writer and had to learn his orchestration by emulation of his predecessors. The piano remains, in the end, a natural tool on which he worked but not an ultimate means of expression except where it most expressively works as accompaniment.

Schubert's piano music then is not the primary product of a virtuoso pianist writing for the fulfilment of his demanding capacities, borne out by the fact that he never ventured into the concerto field, as was natural to such skilled exponents as Mozart, Beethoven and Hummel. Such music generally clothes itself in its own conceits, decorations and built-up harmonies, according to the ability of the performer. Very little of Schubert's piano music is virtuoso in this sense. We do not face the appalling difficulties of Liszt's music, for example, or even the neat dexterity of Mozart's. There are tricky passages and much beyond average competence, but it mainly stays within certain bounds and much of it appears unclothed and unpolished, except in isolated smaller works. It has something of the nature of accompanying music striking out in its own right.

Diligent attempts have been made in recent years, both by writers and performers, to persuade us that Schubert's sonatas are great piano music. Much progress has happily been made in this direction and a gratifyingly widespread amount of attention by leading virtuoso pianists has been dedicated to the piano sonatas. It has at least convinced us that they were perhaps better than had been supposed; without going so far as to elevate them to masterpieces of the genre or to persuade us that Schubert was a naturally pianistic composer. Much of the music has a suggestion of being a sketch for something greater. He often wrote piano sketches for chamber and orchestral works which, provocatively, has often led to the general assumption that certain piano works were sketches for specific works with which they were not offically connected, for example the Grand Duo for the 'lost' 'Gastein' Symphony.

However, we have come far from the generally accepted opinion of many, clearly expressed by Hubert Parry, that 'Schubert's movements are in varying degree diffuse in form, slip-shod in craftsmanship and unequal in content' with little 'feeling for abstract, design, balance and order'. Such thoughts probably dissuaded many pianists of the mid-nineteenth century from including Schubert sonatas in their programmes. In fact, most of the claims can still be substantiated if, as is the underlying import of it all, we compare the Schubert sonatas with an orderly set of compositions like Beethoven's. His sonatas, it should be noted, tended to move from strict sonata form to something much looser in the end, fast approaching the fantasia. Mozart, earlier, had occasionally taken a much freer approach; for instance, starting his lovely No. 4 in E flat with an expressive adagio movement; whereas many of the later sonatas are surprisingly formal in shape. Schubert tended to keep to the same route, experimenting earlier but seeming to enjoy acceptance of the strict sonata form later. The real objection to the Schubert sonatas at that early stage was based on a lack of appreciation of the kind of individual composer that Schubert was – an experimenter, a romantic soul in a classical world. By now we can say, with Richard Capell and others, that not to have had the Schubert sonatas would have been a great loss to music. Their very number and substance made them a force that eventually had to be reckoned with, far outweighing the contribution to the sonata repertoire of many pianistic composers who were more highly rated. It was not until the twentieth century, with writers like Tovey, that some approval of the sonatas began to move pianists towards their performance. He found in them little formal development but a fascinating exploration of key relationship. The more we know of Schubert, even in his lighter works, the more revealing this approach becomes. The real criticism is that Schubert, wandering through his changes and modulations, pursuing his fingered thoughts in an improvisatory way, often did not bother about cool classical logic. Soon pianists – Schnabel was one – were beginning to play the sonatas. Yet even by the beginning of the LP age their appearance on record was fitful. What finally swayed the balance in their favour, however, were the increasing number of 'great' performances that appeared, even if they were of a selected few. The fact that pianists like Haskil, Solomon, Rubinstein and Curzon could make their chosen sonata sound like a towering masterpiece at last persuaded the world that there was a substantial body of works here that had to be explored. In recent decades 'complete' sets (of varying completeness) have appeared from such balanced exponents as Kempff, Haebler, Badura-Skoda and Brendel, the latter, particularly managing to achieve a high level of inspired interpretation. The best Schubert interpreters, in all fields, but perhaps most noticeably in the piano works, have a reservoir of insatiable virtuosity on tap, like a powerful car with over-drive, but have then had the sense and sensibility to control the possible excesses to which virtuosic display leads. Forgetting too that the sonatas were often thought unpianistic – in the sense that they did not follow the natural dictates of the fingers of a pianist, the pianistic instinct that makes what look like an impossible page of decorative music reasonably surmountable – good quality playing has made them seem more playable.

Altogether Schubert accumulated some twenty-three compositions to which the term 'sonata' has been attached; some of them are, as we might expect, fragmentary. Including some of the better fragments, Maurice Brown considered that twenty of them were worth including in the 'complete' cycle. They range from 1815 to 1828 but the majority are, in fact, from 1817 onward when Schubert was approaching twenty. The sonata was not an early manifestation in the extreme sense, but an 'early' group appear from 1815–17, a maturer group from 1823–26, and finally three considered masterpieces that appeared in a block, like Mozart's last symphonies, D958–60. Maurice Brown finds one of Schubert's finest early inspirations in the Andante of D570–1, a concoction of incomplete movements, which led a separate existence for many years as D604. D568 in E flat offers a small drama of conflicting movements. D664 is a more successful integration of lyrical ideas. Another 'unfinished' masterpiece was the Sonata in C (D840), which Schubert began to write in April 1825, 'one of the outstanding works of the composer's middle years'. It stands, like its equivalent symphony, as a satisfying entity in its two-movement form, with a similar well-architectured first movement, followed by a melodious but substantial andante in C minor. It can be taken as it is with complete satisfaction. Badura-Skoda has recorded it in a complete form which he builds up from Schubert's incomplete sketches.

If there is one sonata that seems a potential masterpiece, and ready to stand alongside Beethoven, it is the final sonata in B flat (D960), which settles into its lengthy form with the informal yet ordered sense of repose and assurance, that we also find in the C major Quintet. Above all he achieves a really satisfactory rounding-off, a true sense of coming to an inevitable end. The 'andante sostenuto' movement stands unashamedly beside the slow movement of the Quintet – which comes from the same period. For those acutely aware of Schubert's adventures in keys, the inspired move to C major near the end before moving through E to the home key of C sharp is remarkably effective.

So we can browse happily through Schubert's sonatas and find many overlooked felicities, and maybe agree with Capell when he said that it would be a pity if all we had of Schubert's piano music were the Impromptus and *Moments musicaux*. It would be a pity to lose any of Schubert's music, but it is perhaps in these miscellaneous pieces for piano, piano duet and two pianos that we will find so much of the essential and realised Schubert, if we are not too ashamed of their open attractiveness.

A tendency to see sequences of formal works, i.e. piano sonatas, string quartets, relating to one another is to a large extent justified. The composer's mind seems to have been pulled towards building on existing foundations and pushing the limits of the chosen form. Such groups are self-perpetuating. On the other hand, the works that stand in greater isolation, using certain forms and titles once or twice, seem both to take on more individuality and to relate more to his musical explorations as a whole; and, in the case of Schubert's works, arising from what seems a fairly illogical sequence of writings, it is the isolated works which seem to contain most strongly the strains that are most clearly identifiable as Schubertian. These are the works that ultimately make most poetic impact, though very often they are the ones least praised by the musicologist, i.e. such chamber works as the Piano Quintet and the Piano Trios. Amongst his piano repertoire such items are frequent and fascinating because they hold so much of the genetic nature of his music. Schubert appears to use the piano, as we might expect, as an improvisational outlet, letting his mind speak through his fingers and producing music which is most allied to his inner nature. This applies also to the sonatas, but produces more concentrated poetry in the shorter and more individual works.

Most of all this individualism comes out in the solo piano works which were mainly written for his own intimate performances among appreciative friends who were not particularly highbrow in their musical inclinations. Most of his close circle, as remarked elsewhere, were literary and artistic rather than musical. Schubert had written a considerable body of sonatas before the 1820s, and a few isolated piano pieces (presumably many are still lost for good) that were simply movements of incompleted sonatas, plus the few obligatory sets of variations in which composers traditionally limbered up. Sets of variations, even in the hands of great exponents such as Haydn and Mozart, tend to be slightly academic in appeal. It was Beethoven who, above all, was able to organise such a technical exercise into a romantic whole as in the *Eroica* and *Diabelli* variations. Schubert, not particularly inclined to virtuosic display, is fairly unadventurous but often effective in the Ten Variations of 1815 (D156) on a song-like theme, and the thirteen on a theme by Anselm Hüttenbrenner (D576). We find Schubert retreating into poetry in his response to the famous Diabelli request for a variation from fifty-one different composers. He changed the major theme into the minor and produced an exquisitely tender piece of typical Schubertian lyricism (D718).

Once only, in the solo piano field, did Schubert really move into the realms of extrovert virtuosity and this was in the remarkable *Wanderer* Fantasia of 1825 (D760), written in proximity to the 'Unfinished' Symphony and demonstrating the same elevated mode of thought. It is in essence a sonata that has thrown over all the bonds of discipline, with four sections that bear some relationship to the conventional four movements of a sonata but are played continuously, and amount to what might be called a pianistic tone-poem. The theme is based on the song of the same name, openly used in the slow section where it moves most closely to its song form. Like the 'Unfinished' Symphony, it is a work of tremendous power and daring which Schubert rarely equalled outside the song-cycles. The type of music to which it belongs was moved towards, but not equalled in, his other two fantasias for violin and piano (D934) and piano duet (D940), works of his 'maturity'. The composition is remarkable for the way in which its diverse elements are worked into a dramatic whole: the opening allegro, of a comparatively straightforward symphonic character, moving into the C sharp minor adagio where the *Wanderer* theme is the basis of a flowing set of variations which lead us to E major. The lively 'presto scherzo' fairly bursts with life; finally modulating back to C and a dazzling fugal treatment of the main subject. That this work led to what was virtually a new art form, the symphonic-poem, which was to be the descendent of the formal symphony in the late nineteenth century, is confirmed by the remarkable success and power of Liszt's orchestral treatment of the work *c.* 1851. It is true that some of the poetical element disappears as Liszt steps up the dynamic power of the work, so that it ends up as a cross between a tone-poem and a full-scale concerto, a remarkable hint of what Schubert might have achieved with further orchestral experience and the ambitions of a concert pianist. The nearest he got, otherwise, to a 'concerto' was the strange '*Notturno*' (D897).

At the centre of Schubert's achievement as a pianistic composer come the two sets of Impromptus (D899 and D835) and their considered coda, the three *Klavierstücke* (D946), also designated impromptus. This title (later utilised by Chopin) was probably given to the first set by the publisher, rather than Schubert, and he is in flagrant conflict with the textbook definition of an impromptu which tends to deny their improvisatory qualities; which, in spite of their ultimate polish and tidiness of presentation, they still strongly possess. We can only guess at Schubert's intentions as he wrote these pieces. He was not the originator of the impromptu, although he wrote his when the name had just come into fashion. (Liszt had written an *Impromptu brillant* on operatic themes in 1824 and a set of Impromptus by Vorisek had been published in Vienna in 1822.) So we cannot be clear as to what Schubert intended or had been inspired by when he wrote the first set of these works to which he gave no particular name. Schumann's later assertion that the second set, at least, were intended as the four movements of a sonata has generally been contradicted, but it is not all that far-fetched. The same slightly independent character of each movement is to be found in many four movement works by Schubert; while the compulsive interest in key relations adds to the logic of regarding the pieces as whole. The second set, published as Op. 142 after Schubert's death, moved from F minor to A flat and B flat and back to F minor. Schubert's own numbering of them as Nos. 5 to 8 shows, however, that he intended them as separate pieces and a sequel to Nos. 1–4, which are also entirely in flat keys (though the publisher originally changed the third G flat impromptu to G to make it simpler to play). In his usual way, Schubert was unconcerned as to whether they were all published together or separately.

The first of the D899 set in C minor is the nearest in character to a sonata movement, opening with a declamatory phrase which hangs in the air throughout all the pieces. It is, however, more of a set of variations on two linked themes, one in the major, one in the minor, ending in a long coda in which they become less separately defined. The second Impromptu is marked in E flat but soon wanders into a minor vein and modulates firmly into B minor for most of its time. It has been pointed out that such a swiftly rippling piece well suits the description of Schubert's playing by one of his friends, who said his fingers 'ran over the keyboard like mice'. The third Impromptu in G flat is something of a nocturne with the flowing quality of the stream that Schubert was so attracted to in his songs. Mendelssohn would no doubt have seen it as a 'song-without-words'. The fourth Impromptu is perhaps one of the most quintessentially Schubertian pieces we have. Perhaps he started this one after playing some Clementi for the descending arpeggios, with an awkward repetition of the same note on the fourth and fifth quavers, are typical of many of his sonatas. The opening section, perversely starting in the minor before settling into the major key of A flat, has a split personality with the cascading arpeggios constantly underlined by the broadly folky kind of theme that is present in so many of his song accompaniments. It tails off with a semi-cadenza into a completely contrasting centre section, full of his most chromatic harmonies, with another kind of song character altogether, the probing, wandering kind rather than the classically linear. Like a rocket ascending, a thin line of notes moves into top gear and back to the arpeggio section repeated, through minor to major, and with a neatly rounded-off ending. Nothing could be more distinctively Schubertian. If these four impromptus could really be regarded as a sonata, what a sonata it would be, with an unbeatable finale. It was the next set, however, that prompted Schumann's remark. The mood here is rather more consistent and they are more formally balanced. The third movement is again one of those quintessentially Schubertian inventions, a delightful set of variations on that beloved theme from *Rosamunde*, also used again as the basis of the slow movement of the A minor String Quartet (D804). This is not only richly independent Schubertian thinking but also the basis of what must be one of the best written sets of variations ever conceived by Schubert or anyone else, alight with imaginative touches. Alfred Einstein saw these works as Schubert's ultimate achievement as a piano composer. The spontaneous quality of his best music is joyfully attained throughout, spiced with the right degree of expressive probing and technical experiment. Inspiration of the moment sits upon them in holy innocence. It is Schubert being entirely himself.

In his last year Schubert wrote three more pieces (D946) which may well have been intended as the start of another set of impromptus – and are often so-called. Delightful as they are and interesting to play they never achieve quite the same spontaneous feel nor do they have a partner to match the A flat impromptu of the first set or the B flat of the second. Perhaps that was the one to come. A profound sadness lies over them all and they may never attain the same public popularity as their predecessors, although they are highly rated by many pianists, amongst them Claudio Arrau.

The six *Moments musicaux* (D780) might be seen as a preparatory warm-up, in slighter form, for the Impromptus. They are probing pieces, just removed by their size from the dances. Again they have one member of the sextet who represents the irrepressible writer of popular melodies that is Schubert behind the desire and accepted destiny of being a great composer. And they pose, as the impromptus do, the 'overwhelming question' as to what Schubert's real aims were: to probe the soul or simply to beautify the world with harmonic grace. The two flighty Scherzos of 1817 are in the same category.

And then we come to the elusive, fey world of the 'collected' dances – two whole volumes of them, some 400 items altogether. It is inevitable to wonder why so many of these 'trifles' should be committed to paper. It is also inevitable to note that Mozart dabbled in assorted dances in much the same way, not simply as an apprentice task or a *jeu d'esprit* but right through his composing career, most remarkably penning a veritable spate of them in the final years while he was writing some of his most substantial masterpieces. Schubert likewise scattered these 'trifles' or 'gems' (whichever way we choose to look at them) throughout his working career. There is no clear reason why. We know that it was his pleasure to improvise such pieces at the various dances and soirées that he attended either amongst friends or as a working entertainer. He obviously enjoyed doing it and it had its rewards. He would improvise these dances endlessly and if one particularly pleased him he would try it again, commit it to memory and eventually write it down. Later some of them proved saleable, though not effectively more than his other works. The best collection of them, the *Original Tänze* (later called *Erste Walzer*) (D365) was published in 1821 in two volumes, amongst his earliest published works, being a collection of thirty-six pieces written between 1816 and 1821. These became very popular, with No. 2, the *Trauerwalzer*, having a strange life of its own. The next set (D366) *17 Deutsche Tänze* (or *Ländler*) were mainly unpublished till 1869, long after his death. Another collection of *12 Walzer, 17 Ländler und 9 Ecossaisen* (D145) was published in 1823 and another of *16 Deutsche Tänze und Ecossaisen* (D783) in 1825. The publishers Diabelli adopted currently fashionable titles in 1825 with *34 Valses sentimentales* (D779) in 1825 and the *Valses nobles* (D969) which appeared in 1827, amongst other scattered publications. So there was some practical reason for the continual production of such pieces.

But we might also look for more personal and subjective reasons; first, that writing such slight and undemanding thoughts down is a pleasant enough way of relieving the strain of larger works; second, in regarding them as a sort of prolonged sketch-book of ideas. This particularly gives weight to the hypothetical notion of Schubert as a popular composer. When *Das Dreimädelhaus* and *Lilac Time* went their 'body-snatching' ways, it was this endless storehouse of living melodies that most consistently provided material. These despised works are mentioned again simply to muse on the possibilities of Schubert himself having used them in such a fashion. What wonderful operetta material they would have made. But perhaps he was ahead of his time in this respect. Certainly, in retrospect, we can see Schubert's moulding of the Viennese waltz strain as of tremendous importance to the foundation of the popular Viennese dance school. Mozart's similar pieces had a more classical flavour to them. Schubert's, with that final ingredient of the Italian and Tyrolean flavour, are quite firmly of the popular Viennese tradition, obvious Schrammel quartet material. They are true waltzes, rather than minuets, and they gave the final push to a tradition started by Haydn and Mozart, pursued by Beethoven and Dittersdorf in a rather Germanic sort of way (the sublime effectiveness of the *Eroica* dance theme is an exceptional success), which led to Schubert's path by way of such collections as Hummel's *Tänze für die Apollo-Sale* (1808). Mosco Carner, in his short study *The Waltz*, pins them down neatly: 'These Schubert dances best illustrate the style of the early-nineteenth-century Viennese waltz. Many still breathe a rustic air, the air of the Wiener Wald, the country round Vienna ... Hybrids between *Ländler* and true waltz, they reflect the *Gemütlichkeit*, the homely atmosphere of the *Biedermeier*.' They were certainly the basic material for the extended waltzes of Lanner and the Strausses (who must have known them well) and for all that followed in the Viennese dance world. Carner goes on to say:

> Their charm and beauty is often thrown into greater relief by Schubert's unexpected modulations and his choice of the most delicate harmonies, some of which are truly prophetic of Schumann, Chopin and Wagner, notably those of his twelve *Ländler*, Op. 171 (D790). And it is surprising what variety of mood the composer manages to express within the short-winded form and under the tyranny of three-four rhythm. The gay, robust and rumbustious peasant element here mixes with the sentimentality of *Biedermeier*, and the sad, feminine sweetness of Schubert's own nostalgia. Lanner and Strauss never wrote a waltz in a minor key; it would have seemed a paradox to them. Yet some of Schubert's most inspired dances

> are in the minor, and of a poetic beauty and poignancy rarely rivalled by any of the later concert waltzes. Schubert knew that nothing is sadder than a sad waltz.

It was Weber, rather than Schubert, who led the way to the big work in 3/4 with his famous *Invitation to the Dance* of 1819, though Schubert himself clearly employed his own experiences in such movements as the scherzo of the C major Symphony.

An understanding of the effect and purpose of these small but polished gems seems to fascinate some musicians and elude others. Stravinsky, for instance, a lover of miniatures, played them endlessly and admired their grace and ingenuity. He reports that Scriabin, however, thought them 'only good to be rendered on the piano by schoolgirls'. Rachmaninov had no high regard either and Debussy described them as 'inoffensive stuff – redolent of the bottom drawers of provincial old maids'.

The delightful and endlessly rewarding set D365 stands as a supreme example of the care and thought that went into these pieces. A theme for what almost amounts to a set of variations is laid down in the first waltz in A flat – a perfect statement of a melodic idea in eight bars; followed by a straight switch to F (not even a modulation) to begin the second eight which apologetically moves back by way of B flat to the original A flat. The next waltz, the famous *Trauerwalzer*, is also in A flat (in its original form) but practically gets into the sharp keys of B and A before sliding back to A flat again. Just to show what could be done. The experiments continue in A flat with No. 12 a true Alpine sort of dance. By No. 14 we are in D flat, but No. 16, which is a subtle variation of No. 1, is in A. Now we have a period in the sharp keys, G, E, D and A all exploited, before, at No. 31 (Atzenbrugger Deutsche No. 6), we are in a curiously unpoised C. And now a strange but highly effective ending with No. 33 a boisterous piece in F (which modulates in the middle to A flat – the very opposite to No. 1), followed by the lightly Chopinesque No. 34, which should surely be played slowly and delicately, with the oddly awkward No. 35 leading to a statement of the folk-tune *Bruderlein fein* which Schubert rounds off with a superbly chorded coda and a meditative ending. Was he saying that this haunting tune was really the basis of it all, or was it just a theatrical stroke? The possibilities of interpreting this set are immense. Some simply select their own suite and this is often effective. You can take or reject the repeats with telling effect. Variety of mood and pace are essential.

At No. 2 stands the justifiably popular *Trauerwalzer* which is certainly to be reckoned amongst Schubert's hit tunes. Maurice Brown devoted a fascinating piece in his *Essays on Schubert* to the adventures of this particular morsel, which typifies, in many ways, the Schubertian misadventure. Its charm and poise hoisting it head and shoulders above the run-of-the-mill dances by lesser writers, it achieved wide local popularity in Vienna from the time that Schubert first played it somewhere around 1816 – or possibly before. He jotted it down in several places, first as a few scribbled bars on the manuscript of a song. Someone nicknamed it the *Trauerwalzer* and it soon became so well-known that it was mistakenly, but justifiably, looked upon as a folk-tune. Schubert confirmed it as his own by making several copies for such friends as Anselm Hüttenbrenner, each time describing it as 'Deutscher' and writing it in A flat with occasional small variations in its melodic line. So far, in each case, the opening note before the main eight bars was a single E flat. It seems that very soon the whole of Vienna was going around humming this tune which must at least have given Schubert some satisfaction. His only comment, however, on being told that people called it the *Trauerwalzer*, the 'mourning' or 'mournful' waltz, was 'what idiot would compose a mournful waltz?' In 1820 a Viennese dance composer, Johann Pensel, appearing to believe in all honesty that it was a folk-tune, published a set of variations for the piano on the *beliebten Trauerwalzer*. In 1821 another set of variations appeared on the *beliebten Wiener-Walzer*, this time by Carl Czerny and apparently still in honest ignorance of the source of this 'anonymous' melody. Then in 1821 came the publication, by Diabelli, of Schubert's Op. 9 (D365) set in which it appears as No. 2 with its nickname firmly printed above it and accepted by Schubert. By then he had changed the opening E flat to a 3-note E flat, D natural, E flat phrase that now seems most natural to it. It was Czerny's fame, however, which carried the waltz beyond Vienna, when his variations were published in London in 1823. A reviewer in a London periodical called the waltz 'graceful and expressive', becoming the first Englishman to write on Schubert, albeit without mention of his name. By 1825 the Czerny piece was in Paris as variations on '*une Valse Viennoise favorite*', likewise in Germany, and again in London in 1827, where once more the beautiful subject of the variations got favourable comment. There had also been various arrangements published by Diabelli in the meantime, and others which attributed the waltz itself to Czerny. Typically, there was not a word uttered on the subject by Schubert. Even more oddly, Beethoven's name was being connected with the waltz by 1825. It was published by Schott of Mainz in 1826 as *Le Desir: Walzer favorit* by Beethoven with another section, by an unacknowledged hand, tacked on to it. Beethoven is said to have protested, but perhaps Schubert enjoyed having one of his works attributed to Beethoven. Furthermore, Schott then published it with words and a piano and guitar accompaniment, which at last drew an angry protest from Schindler about 'two waltzes with verses fitted; the first is by J. Schubert and the second by Hummel'. It was later assumed that he meant F. Schubert and Himmel; but whatever it was, it had little effect. Strangely the additional bars are quite possibly by Schubert as well. Schott pursued their wicked ways in 1828 by publishing a miscellany of *6 Valses et une Marche funèbre* as a '*Souvenir à Louis van Beethoven*'. None of the pieces, which were often reprinted (they are still to be found in a Peters 'Salon-Album' of *c.* 1870) were by Beethoven and Schubert's waltz appeared as *Sehnsuchts-Walzer* (a German equivalent of '*désir*'). This was the title accepted by Schumann and others who tried to put matters right in various publications in the 1830s. By 1826, when Czerny's variations were republished in Vienna, Fr. Schubert was, in fact, being attributed. By 1829, just after Schubert's death, some writers had begun to query his rights to the piece anyway and there were suggestions that he had stolen the theme from some obscure operetta. Others suggested its source was to be found in composers as varied as Haydn or Beethoven, on the one hand, and Hoffmann, Henneberg, Schnabel and Strub on the other. All these theories were mentioned in Kreissle's biography of Schubert. Josef Hüttenbrenner is mentioned as the chief counsel for the defence of Schubert's rights to the piece. In fact, a similar theme does occur in Beethoven's E flat Sonata, Op. 7, which *could* have been a subconscious spur to Schubert's thoughts. The publication of the piece in every possible variant form, title and attribution continued through the nineteenth century. One publisher printed a footnote apology to Czerny for his waltz having been attributed to Beethoven. Grove gave the piece a special entry in his *Dictionary* in order to give Schubert his final due. Most publishers, particularly those who contributed the various song versions (such as Richault of Paris, who also invented a Schubert song called *Adieu*) adopted Schubert's name as soon as it had its own drawing power, but continued to print the piece with its doubtful additional section. Finally, of course, it became the main song of the operetta pastiches and thus finally damned itself in the eyes of purist critics. Out of all this, one is only left regretting that Schubert himself had so little share in the fame of this casual gem, probably conceived in a few pensive moments.

If Schubert appears as a fitful composer of normal two-handed piano pieces, he appears, in contrast, as perhaps one of the most prolific of all writers in the field of four-hand, piano duet, music. In this case the reason is simple and logical. Most of his duet music was for pupils, such as the Esterházys, to perform with their teacher. Contrary to a possible expectation that such music would tend to be less profound than the solo music, it produced some pieces of particularly profound and solid worth. Perhaps it was in this manner that Schubert could out-write his own capacities as a pianist, allotting part of the difficulties to another player. Whatever the reason, his piano music for two is a remarkable body of work which is only now being given the full attention that it deserves. It includes a number of dances, some 'overtures', rondos, sets of variations, and a number of miscellaneous works that are of passing interest. But it also contains many substantial works that are even nearer to the symphonic spirit than the solo piano music. Among the works only recently given much attention are the once popular *Divertissement à la hongroise* (D818) and the mistakenly fragmented *Divertissement sur des motifs français* (D823). The first became a familiar Schubertian item on the days when his music was still selectively admired, attracting drawing-room attention because of its contrasting fashionable Hungarian themes and sentimental cantabile passages. Written at Zseliz, it was supposedly based on a tune that Schubert heard a peasant girl singing while he was out walking one day. It is a friendly sort of work in *Rosamunde* vein, as is the less popular French piece. But at least three of the four-handed works stand out as mature Schubert masterpieces: the *Grand Duo* (Sonata in C major) (D812); the *Fantasia* in F minor (D940); and the *Allegro* in A minor (D947). These are complemented by such convincing pieces as the *Grand Rondeau* in A (D951) and several others. Such music was more or less as much second nature to him as his chamber works. A Fantasia in G of 1810 is the first item in the Deutsch catalogue.

The *Grand Duo*, the published title of the Sonata in C, written at Zseliz in April 1824, is a large ambitious work. It has long been considered to display an 'orchestral' mode of thought and style, which led to Schumann's suggestion that it was perhaps an arrangement of a symphony, and to the various assumptions that it was indeed the lost 'Gastein' Symphony, neatly written out (and indeed it possessed a particularly neat manuscript, which might simply be a second copy) with features such as sustained octaves, which Tovey found objectionable in pure piano music, pointing to its orchestral source. The orchestral element, seems, on objective examination, to be over-exaggerated. There is little or nothing to be found in this sonata that cannot be found in the other, often thickly written, piano works of Schubert. For once Schubert himself makes several mentions of the work and firmly comes down on the side of the pragmatist who sees it purely as a piano work by referring to it as a 'sonata' with no hint of any dark hidden secrets. It has been orchestrated by Karl Salomon, Anthony Collins and Joachim, Collins finding it necessary to explain at points that it was, in fact, pure keyboard music which had to be reinforced in his arrangements. The Joachim orchestration makes a good case for the labour involved, but does not prove to the sceptic anything other than that much of Schubert is good material for such treatment, underlining his orchestral deficiencies. Even for two pianists it is an impressive work, though, and is in a typical Schubertian idiom, close textured, full of four-part writing and bold harmonies. In fact, it is simply Schubert in the introspective mood that we more often discover in his chamber music.

In perspective, Schubert's piano duet music is simply an intermediate step between his solo works and his chamber music.

5 CHAMBER MUSIC

The string quartet, and its near relatives in chamber music, were the kind of music that Schubert breathed naturally. He was brought up to its repertoire, playing with the family quartet, of which he very soon took charge, admonishing the others, including his father who was inclined to be a careless musician, and so growing up with an early appreciation of the works then available in this genre. It showed him another dimension beyond the keyboard and he generally played the violin or viola himself in such ensembles. Not surprisingly, then, the string quartet was prominent amongst his early works, mixed with an immediate and fluent output of songs, the second item in the Deutsch catalogue being a fragment of a String Quartet in G dated *c.* 1810, and the third being three movements of a quartet which was first performed in the Schubert household around 1811.

The first fully accredited quartet, called No. 1 in the Breitkopf & Härtel Complete Edition, Series V, of 1890 and the Deutsch chronology*, is specified as a String Quartet in Mixed Keys (D18). This work composed in 1812, was written while Schubert was a pupil at the Konvikt where he played violin in the orchestra. Its mixing of keys produces a rather strange wandering piece (not without attractive moments) moving through somewhat wayward modulations that are interesting as the experiments of a schoolboy hand. The second Quartet in C (D32) is an early essay in the art of remaining unfinished. The Presto was completed on 30 September 1812 and a Minuet and Trio, Andante and Allegro finale are assumed to make up the rest of its structure. After domestic performance it lay on a publisher's shelf for years, slowly disintegrating and the third movement and most of the fourth disappeared. It was first published in 1890 as a two-movement work. The slow movement was later rediscovered and is assumed to be identical with one of the movements listed by Deutsch as D3. It is, like all Schubert's apprentice efforts, a pleasant enough piece that is clearly influenced by Haydn and Mozart. Such works as *Die Zauberflöte*, the late Mozart symphonies, Haydn's dance movements and Beethoven symphonies lend constant reminiscent strains to many of these early quartets. No. 3 in B flat (D36) shows the influence of the school and his teachers in its rather self-conscious essays in counterpoint. The manuscript bears markings in Salieri's handwriting. The loosely grouped early quartets 1–7 and No. 10 (which was originally dated 1817–24 but, on discovery of the manuscript, was found to bear the date 1813) are all pleasantly traditional works, full of points of interest and moments of charm, not confirmed in the Schubertian vein but continually full of hints of his musical personality. Most writers seem to have considered them minor works.

The 'inner unity' that is expected of a chamber work is first discerned by the Schubert authority Walther Vetter, writing in

* 'The Chronology of Schubert's String Quartets' by Otto Deutsch in *Music and Letters*, Vol. 34, 1943.

1934, in No. 8 in B flat (D112). Schubert had set out to write a trio but after writing ten bars as such changed his mind and started again in quartet form. He records that the first movement was eventually written in four and a half hours. Vetter further notes some evidence of Beethoven's Sixth Symphony having had an influence and finds its first principal theme possessed of that 'endless' nature that is to be a clear trademark of many of the more distinctive chamber works. Einstein finds clear traces of Mozart quartets in the 'Andante sostenuto', but overall finds the 'blissful' nature of true Schubertian themes beginning to emerge and, as we have often seen before, a finale that has an entirely individual vivacity and wit, with many motifs of the 'Great' C major Symphony's scherzo already there in embryo form. It is significant to remember that Schubert, at this point, already had the First Symphony written and was about to embark upon the Second, both of which are notable for their final movements. D112 is a remarkably assured work, if viewed in isolation; a firm step forward in the quartet saga, if seen in perspective. The discovery of the later scherzo in unresolved (in hindsight) chamber-music form in the finale of this quartet is really something of a shock to the Schubert researcher.

It is nothing short of uncanny to find, on the one hand, that these themes had already been discovered by him as early as 1814; on the other hand, that he should still find fulfilment in using themes of 1814 as the material of one of his greatest works. Were they even a conscious lift or did he simply return to familiar work patterns in 1824 (or wherever we ultimately place the symphony)? It is not only a curious reflection on the involved workings of Schubert's genius but of the whole process of musical creation. Even so prolific a composer as Schubert only achieves a limited number of basic themes with an extra-musical life to them. Here is one idea that was surely basic to his creative thoughts.

From now on it becomes clearer that Schubert was making more progress toward a final style in his chamber music than in any other form he tackled. It was here that the essential lyricism of his song-writing was to be most completely absorbed into instrumental writing. Quartet No. 9 in G minor (D173) takes two important steps forward; first, and probably least important, in coming to terms with the formal construction of the quartet and the thematic links between the movements, with much of the thematic material inspired by Mozart in his G minor vein (notably the Symphony – one of Schubert's favourite works); second, in the presentation of the typically Schubertian movement in which the music appears to unfold like a flower. In the slow movement (andantino) particularly there is a sort of probing dialogue between first violin and cello, with the other two instruments providing a persistent accompaniment that is essentially the art of his *Lieder* writing brought to fruition in the string quartet. Closely matched to this work is the next Quartet No. 11 in E major (D353) which has the same probing nature.

Up to this point, in spite of the subtle additions he was beginning to make to the form, Schubert was simply walking in the steps of Mozart. In the E major quartet it is *Figaro* and the late symphonies that spark off his ideas. After this there is a significant gap in his quartet writing activities that can only leave us speculating. These years produced the Fourth, Fifth and Sixth Symphonies but predominantly they were filled with vocal music of many kinds, mainly songs of all shapes and sizes. Two String Trios of 1816 (D471) and 1817 (D581) are rarely played or recorded and seem to be rather half-hearted pieces, though pleasant enough. Apart from these the most significant work in the present context is the Piano Quintet in A, the famous and much-loved 'Trout' Quintet. What was the impetus that impelled the creation of this oddly isolated masterpiece? Its instrumentation, as mentioned earlier, was simply the result of that particular line-up, notably the inclusion of a double-bass, being available during the musical diversions of a happy holiday in the Austrian Alps in 1819. It was written probably without much deep thought but with technical assurance and for the entertainment of friends. The learned observers have generally decried its sunny and open nature as if chamber music was never ordained for enjoyment. They say it is not a great work and some take exception to the inclusion of the bass in a quintet. That is only allowed in larger ensembles. The piano part is in the reigning conventions of the day, the variation style, and even in the work's more solemn moments, e.g. the F sharp minor portion of the andante, it lapses into frivolity. Its structure has been described as 'mechanical'. There is perhaps little by way of thoughtful development. J.A. Westrup goes so far as to suggest that we might as well drink and talk through a performance of it, so simple and merely enjoyable is its nature, and he finds *Die Forelle* a curious choice for the variations movement. Now all this, of course, is part of that critical defensive hedge that tries to hide the fact that Schubert was partly a great popular composer. It was part of the late nineteenth and twentieth century conspiracy of seriousness, the almost religious belief, which the Victorians started, that music is only great and good if it is obscurely profound and with a solemnity that results from mental anguish. The annoying thing about the 'Trout' Quintet is that it was clearly written in such a burst of primitive enthusiasm and good-nature that it broke from the bonds of seriousness that even Schubert stayed within for most of his quartet writing, and produced the one piece of chamber music that is universally enjoyed. Your standpoint depends on whether you believe that most great composers would not have written it even if they could or that they could not even if they tried. In the end, we simply have to accept that Schubert was a musical split-personality. There was the serious and searching composer of the String Quintet and *Winterreise* (although even there he could scarcely restrain the feathered songster within him); and there was the true son of Vienna who found perpetual joy in melody and could not hold back the strain of pure lyricism. The 'Trout' Quintet is a flood of musical optimism and tunefulness, a profligate use of material that many would spread over a dozen works and it is in top inspirational gear all the time. And, as so often happens with Schubert, he would later take a little from this gold-mine of melody and add it to some further musical concoction or use some of it to shape one of his 'popular' songs like 'Who is Sylvia?'.

So one senses in Schubert's musical progress the private tug-of-war that ultimately did as much as anything to keep him in obscurity. Publishers often found him too progressive; the serious musical establishment often found him too frivolous; the few nearest to him, who understood, found him simply to be Schubert, a unique phenomenon. Schubert himself had to have foundations, as any composer must. These he found in Haydn and Mozart. He admired Beethoven but knew that he was not of that mighty calibre. He seems to have drifted towards Beethoven as if on a tide, but continually made the effort to swim back to the solid banks. Looked at historically, we may now see Schubert searching for a musical substance that was not to be fully realised until after his death by other composers. It was purely a matter of expression, of notes, harmony and rhythm combining into a whole that was greater than their parts. The search was halted for a while as he mused on how he could take these steps forward at the same time as not losing the natural spirit that was his alone. The next quartet writing to move into our sights like a distant star is, almost predictably, one of those elusive and ineffable fragments that suggests this ongoing turmoil and search: the probing allegro assai in C minor (D703) that is generally known under the ugly but functional German title of *Quartettsatz*. It was probably performed as a one-movement work privately in 1821 but the intention of a complete quartet to come is indicated in an attached forty-one bars of an andante movement in A flat. Like the existing portions of the 'Unfinished' Symphony, we are left with the impression of a movement of such intensity that the composer simply felt unable to match it with more of such quality. Einstein describes the work, in its suggestive key as 'not pathetic but uncanny, the sense of mystery being intensified by the almost continuous tremolo in the "accompaniment" or in the theme itself'. Foreshadowing the A flat of the unwritten andante, the second theme moves into this key rather than ones that might be expected in a classical quartet such as C major or E flat major. It is from beginning to end a seeking, probing, shadowed piece of writing that has simpler predecessors but nothing that we can name that has such a totally weird quality. The interpretative demands of the writing, the freedom of such an instrument as the cello newly released from its accompanying part, suggest music that is no longer being written for amateur performance but asking much of its interpreter, regardless of whether such an interpreter currently existed.

At this point Schubert seems to have realised his course. In a letter to Leopold Kupelwieser (dated 31 March 1824) he wrote: 'I have written few new songs, but I have tried my hand at several instrumental works and have composed two quartets for violins, viola and cello and an octet. I want to write another quartet for this is how I intend to prepare the way to a grand symphony'. So we have in his own words that quartet writing was very much a limbering up for orchestral thoughts; and, as might be concluded, piano writing was an initial exercise for instrumental writing. Much as we might be mystified by Schubert's shifts of mood and form, and his divided intentions, we must at least admit that he was consistent in character and working method.

The two quartets were the two fine works that we know as the A minor (D804) and the D minor (D810) that is known as the 'Death and the Maiden' quartet. Schubert intended these and the projected third to be a set (which would have been published as his Op. 29). The A minor achieved publication as Op. 29, No. 1 but there the project ended, and it remained the only quartet to get into print during his lifetime. It was performed in the Musikverein on 14 March 1824 by the Ignaz Schuppanzigh Quartet and played, in the composer's opinion, as reported by Schwind, rather too slowly but with appropriate purity and tenderness. Schwind found the work gentle and full of expressive melody, especially enjoying the minuet. Two press comments offer contrasting opinions. One rightly said that one would have to hear the work several times to judge it properly (and that is always a good thing to have said about any work); the other (with forgivable lack of information at his disposal, writing in Leipzig) that for a 'first' effort it was not to be despised. It was only the first to be performed in public. There is, quite simply, a sense of realisation in this quartet. It is pure Schubert and, like so many of his quintessential and great works, it draws unashamedly on material from the past that has the mark of personal quality. The theme of the andante is the one that became best known as the third Entr'acte of *Rosamunde* (but had an earlier existence) and which was to be used yet again as the subject of a fine set of variations in the third Impromptu of the second set (D935). The main theme of the minuet is based on his 1819 song to words by Schiller, *Schöne Welt, wo bist du?* The D minor Quartet, also started in 1824, was tinkered with until the beginning of 1826 and had its first performance privately at the home of Josef Barth in Vienna on 1 February 1826 after two rehearsals on 29 and 30 January. During the rehearsals Schubert was still making adjustments, amending instrumental parts and making a cut in the first movement. It was then played again at Franz Lachner's house later in February. The first violinist was the aged professional Schuppanzigh who makes one of those best-forgotten entries into musical history by telling Schubert that the quartet amounted to nothing and that he ought to stick to his song-writing. Schubert is said to have made no comment. He quietly gathered up the parts and later shut them away in his desk with no further thoughts of publication. This lovely work has as its andante a set of variations on his 1817 song, to words by Claudius, *Der Tod und das Mädchen.* It is a work with both sides of Schubert in it: the giving and the asking, and it contains some of his best quartet writing. Schubert, generally speaking, did not write programmatic music so we should not read too much tragic meaning into its sub-title 'Death and the Maiden'. It could even be possible that he started the quartet before he thought of using the song as the basis of the andante. It keeps to a minor key in all its movements and there is a hint of another of his dramatic songs, *Erlkönig*, in the finale. If each movement, as we find in other quartets and the piano sonatas, are satisfying entities in themselves, the only weakness of the whole quartet is that they do not build to an entirely convincing whole. The finale in particular seems to be only loosely connected with the rest and does not complete the symmetry that one would expect of a classical quartet. But that is a facet of Schubert's struggle. If he had gone on to write many more quartets he would perhaps either have written more formally or he would have continued towards the establishment of his own formal enterprises. The glory of the work is undoubtedly the 'Death and the Maiden' movement which has a poise and poignancy that he only occasionally equalled in that small handful of instrumental works that seal his reputation.

Discouraged, perhaps, from further quartet ventures for the moment, the next was not to appear for another two years. While writing the A minor quartet he had also been engaged on a work of a very different nature, the F major Octet for String and Wind Instruments (D803), which is more of the world of the 'Trout' Quintet. It was written for the amateur clarinettist Graf Ferdinand Troyer, at whose lodgings it was probably first played in spring 1824. Its first public performance was not until 16 April 1827 at an Ignaz Schuppanzigh concert at the Musikverein, and it was not published until 1853. Like the 'Trout' and *Die Zwillingsbrüder*, a definite commission seemed to bring out a certain sturdy practicality in the music whose clear strains are given depth by the sheer warmth and richness of its nature. The aim was to write a piece that would add to the repertoire that Beethoven's Septet partly supplied. Like the 'Trout', it is that part of Schubert's music where the outside influence of Rossini might be detected, though Beethoven remains the basic model. His blend of writing for the wind (clarinet, horn and bassoon) and the strings (two violins, viola, cello and double-bass) is pleasantly felicitous and compares well with Mozart's writing in his serenades and divertimenti. Each of the six movements, which follow the pattern set by Beethoven, is perfectly devised. The slow movement (adagio) gives the clarinet its big chance with the main theme and has been compared with the *Ave Maria* setting that Schubert composed a year later. The andante fourth movement is an ingenious set of variations on the duet '*Gelagert unterm hellen Dach der Bäume*' from *Die Freunde von Salamanka*, deployed with a child-like delight in musical games and in very much the same vein as the 'Trout' variations. The minuet has a strangely gentle charm about it. If there is any criticism to be made of the Octet it is that it is more of a suite than a whole work, and that its ingratiatingly summery lightness is possibly too drawn out. It is a long work by any standards, lasting almost an hour. But its mastery of the medium must be measured against the wind writing to be found in the earlier *Eine Kleine Trauermusik* (D79) of 1813 and the Minuet and Finale (D72). Also written in 1824 was that bland but curiously satisfying work, which Schubert penned carelessly, according to Deutsch, as if he cared little for the result, the Arpeggione Sonata (D821). The arpeggione was a strange hybrid instrument with a guitar-shaped body (it was also known as the *guitarre d'amour*, bowed guitar or guitar violoncello – Schubert appears to be the first to call it an arpeggione and the name was only used after his sonata was published). It has six strings tuned, as on a guitar, E, A, D, G, B, E, which pass over a cello-type bridge and are fastened to the kind of tailpiece employed by the violin family, with twenty-four metal frets let into the fingerboard guitar-style, giving it a fully chromatic compass of three octaves E to E. It showed other hereditary likenesses to the cello in having a slightly vaulted rather than flat belly, and it was played with a cello bow. The sound, judged by modern recordings of an original instrument, was nothing more or less than an undernourished cello, though its protagonists speak of a 'beauty, richness and attractiveness of tone'. It presumably failed to catch on greatly because, in spite of its ingenious structure, it was certainly not as flexible or easy to play as the cello and achieved less fluent results. Schubert's piece was first played on the instrument by Vincenz Schuster at a private concert possibly in December 1824. Appended to Schubert's manuscript, held by the Paris Conservatoire, there is a violin part written by another hand and the first publication in 1871 offered alternative versions for cello and violin. Its first public performance in 1871 was on the violin, but since then it has become firmly and affectionately an established part of the cello repertoire, to which instrument it most clearly belongs, and on which we generally hear it played. It is a likeable and straightforward work, gratifying to play both from the cello and piano points of view. Perhaps the work it bears most relation to in Schubert's works is one of his very last, *Der Hirt auf dem Felsen*, a song with piano and clarinet (or cello) accompaniment.

Then in 1826 came his final effort at a String Quartet (No. 15) in G major (D887). As might be hoped, this is a substantial, cohesive work that makes a fitting, if not entirely satisfactory, culmination to Schubert's quartet writing. It had the usual private performance, this time at Lachner's house on 5 March 1827. The first movement only was played at the Vienna Musikverein concert of Schubert's works, the only one that he was involved in or benefited by in his lifetime, on 26 March 1828. Although the quartet was well received, and described by one critic as 'full of spirit and originality', the composer could not persuade anyone to publish it. It has always had less attention than the two attractive and song-based quartets that preceded it, the A minor and D minor, perhaps because it is a long work and is, in fact, less typical of Schubert than the others. It owes much to the Beethoven example. In the complete canon of Schubert's chamber music it must be seen as one of the most questing works of all, a bridge to the final masterpieces, a possible indication of Schubert's partial desire to write deeper and profounder music. What it clearly exhibits is a great assurance in the instrumental writing and a great audacity in its harmonies and modulations. The natural (by that time), sudden but sensuous modulations that are to be found in the dances and elsewhere, have now become considered intellectual exercises. It moves into the world of Beethoven's late quartets and sonatas. It is, in short, one of the least outgoing of all Schubert's writings and occupies a strategic position from which, to the relief of most ardent Schubertians, he withdrew in the works that followed.

In 1827 Schubert produced three works that stand as supreme manifestations of his art and which have attained universal acceptance and admiration. It is curious that, apart from an early venture in 1812 (D28), they are his only essays in the form of Piano Trios. First came an adagio movement in E flat (D897) which it is generally assumed was originally intended to be the second or third movement of a piano trio, maybe a rejected movement of one of the subsequent trios that he produced. On its publication in 1845 it acquired the fashionable title of '*Notturno*' (or 'Nocturne') by which name it is now generally known. It is not entirely suited to its nature. Many Schubert commentators have a fairly low estimate of the piece because it works on a simple basis and wrings dry an attractive theme in a typical 'moto perpetuo' Schubertian way. If, in isolation, it is not a world-shaking composition, it is unquestionably both attractive and intriguing, and stands as a supremely well rounded off sample of his tidal writing; the questing, nudging movement that ebbs and flows rather than developing in any academic sense. It is, moreover, a piece which offers a real interpretative challenge and needs a finely balanced performance to make it a success. It would certainly have made a splendid slow movement to any trio or quartet, and we are left to wonder whether this is yet another unfinished episode which never found the surrounding inspiration, or whether he simply discarded it in favour of other slow movements. Interestingly, it is the one piece of Schubert's piano writing that moves closest to the concerto idiom with a comparatively grandiose part for the instrument. It is a pity that Liszt did not work on it or that Schubert did not have the orchestral ambitions to use it in this manner. Presumably he toyed with the '*Notturno*' as he was writing the B flat Piano Trio (D898).

It is impossible to think of the B flat Trio without considering its younger and profounder brother in E flat (D929) which grew from the same, gradually deepening stream of inspiration. The

B flat Trio, to some degree, delights all admirers of Schubert. It achieves a formal perfection and an instrumental skill that all can admit. It has all the sensitivity and poetry in its central movements that one can hope for, yet basically it is so much in the tuneful *Rosamunde* camp that it is capable of capturing the 'Trout' admirers as well as those seeking profounder stimulus. It has harmonic interest of a unique kind, using chords and inversions of chords that nobody else seems to have quite hit upon before, but they are so deeply woven into the total texture that there is little in it that now startles in any way; and the textures are, indeed, its glories. There is clear linear writing but the blend of the instruments is so close that we must conclude that what Schubert was mostly after was sheer colour, kaleidoscopically changing all the time, but held together by a glorious flow of melody. In the slow movement in particular the writing can only fairly be compared with the inspiration of the 'Unfinished' Symphony. To modern ears the work may seem to be simply an extended impromptu, a carefree exercise, and one cannot escape the impression that Schubert wrote it easily and quickly and in a rosy glow of optimism. Perhaps that is why both he and his assessors find the E flat Trio profounder; which it undoubtedly is. Grove, in the 1882 article in his *Dictionary*, inclined to a view that the two works were written more or less consecutively in October 1827; but Deutsch allows more air between them. Whatever the case, the E flat work is still a logical extension of the B flat. It simply moves into a more serious, less optimistic vein and hence offers a sterner challenge to interpreter and listener alike. While a contemporary performance of the B flat is not mentioned by Deutsch, the E flat was performed by the Schuppanzigh Quartet at the Musikverein on 26 December 1827 and again at the Schubert concert the following March. It also got into print and became the only work by Schubert to be published outside Austria in his lifetime – but only just. The C minor melody of the Andante is said to be based on a Swedish song probably written or arranged by Isaak Albert Berg (as is similarly said of the Andante of the Quartet in G (D887)). He was a folksinger who sang some of his songs to Schubert on a visit to Vienna in 1827. Schubert enjoyed the performance of his Trio and thought it exquisite. The step from the bland beauty of the B flat Trio to the taut drama of the E flat is an important one in our appreciation of Schubert's inward quest. Schumann described the work as 'an angry meteor blazing forth and outshining everything in the musical atmosphere of the time'. The writing in both trios is remarkably similar; the character, as so often in brothers, is startlingly different.

We must always be careful not to be too glib about musical progression but, nonetheless, Schubert's chamber music proves, time and again, a particularly satisfying sphere of his activities, simply because progress is decidedly discernible, a view now greatly clarified by time. The final great chamber work, the String Quintet in C (D956), probably written in August or September 1828, now appears as the apex, the attained climax of all his writings. In fact, the high regard for it has notably grown in our own time. Earlier writers have had their qualifying criticisms of it. Today, it is particularly highly regarded by performers who see it almost as a Holy Grail and the work that most challenges their artistry. Many rate it as the finest chamber music work ever written. Curiously it does not seem to have been particularly important to Schubert for he makes little mention of it in any of his writings (beyond a mention in a letter) and neither do any of his close friends. It was never performed during his lifetime, though Deutsch mentions a rehearsal of it in October 1828. It was not publicly performed until 1850 or published until 1853. There have been suggestions that its two first movements are not matched by the last two and that the work might have been better as an 'Unfinished' Quintet. Or, had Schubert survived his illness and reached that hypothetical maturity, would he perhaps have revised the work from this aspect? The Hungarian-sounding final allegretto (with echoes of the 'Trout') is not, however, a negligible piece and, in order to make these stern judgments at all, one has to take the viewpoint (as proposed by Moser, who saw premonitions of death in the work: a forerunner of all the romantic nonsense written since) that it is a profoundly tragic work. There is surely no conclusive basis for these beliefs. That the work has profundity and weight is without question; yet it also has much of the lighter Schubert in it. It would be fair to say that it is, in fact, one of the works in which Schubert most successfully reconciled the two sides of his creative urge, lending the Schubertian melodic charm the weight of technical assurance and probing musical equations. The slow movement, in particular, is the ultimate example of Schubert's tidal approach. The work as a whole is by no means as deeply serious as, for example, the G major Quartet (No. 15). It is likely that it was, in Schubert's mind, simply a worthy return to the family music-making repertoire with parts for his cellist father and a cello-playing friend and the rest of the family. It is possible that he saw it as little more than this, yet wrote this superb music as a composer with a great weight of chamber music experience behind him. It satisfies the professional musician both by its expressiveness and the rewarding parts for all five instruments, all fully employed throughout its length, and each required to give his utmost to achieve the desired intensity and cumulative beauty of the music. A successful performance (such as the classic one on disc by Casals, Tortelier, Stern, Schneider and Katims which has rarely been equalled) has to have the flow and pulse that comes from absolute togetherness and emotional agreement. Einstein, one of the least critical of Schubert's more perceptive observers, found it so orchestral in conception that it almost went beyond the bounds of chamber music; which is as much a comment on Schubert's orchestral explorations as on this particular work. John Reed simply sees it as 'a supremely poetic expression of the romantic spirit in music' – which is surely where the case may rest. It remains as a fitting last work in this very personal realm of music.

A final word about Schubert's works for the violin. As a violinist himself we might well have expected more both in quantity and quality. It seems that his inclinations here were no more virtuosic than they were with regard to the piano. The three Sonatinas of 1816 (D384, 385, 408) are light and graceful works of great charm but little significance, the first a Mozartian pastiche to all intents and purposes. The A major Sonata of 1817 (D574) is of sturdier stuff, a beautifully rounded, melodic piece that is richly satisfying to perform; likewise the Rondo in B minor (D895) of 1826 and the Fantasie (D934) of 1827. They are all works which are played and recorded by the Schubert enthusiast rather than the violin virtuoso: an exploration of the spirit rather than a fiddler's delight.

6 THE SONGS

Interspersed and spread throughout the whole of his composing life Schubert produced song after song, just over six hundred of them, accounting for much of what, in the light of the Deutsch catalogue, may seem a very large output. However, the whole of Schubert's music gives an impression, true or false, of fairly spontaneous writing and rapid production. Sometimes he wrote a number of songs in one day. If we were to add up the titles that are reasonably well-known it would come to a surprisingly large number, but it still leaves a considerable body of work that is still not widely known or heard; though, in recent years, the bulk of them have been recorded. There is an inclination to think of Schubert as the creator of the German *Lied* and the 'art song' in general. This, of course, is far from the truth. Song has such a long history that a belief that it all happened in the last two hundred years or so is absolute nonsense. Where Schubert did step in was as an innovator of the new romantic *Lieder* where music, rather than being simply a shape to which words were sung, became a creative force alongside and complementary to the words, with the accompaniment no longer just a rhythmic background (though it had long been more than this) but itself an integral part of the composition. If one compares the songs of Mozart with the songs of Schubert the step forward is clearly sensed. Mozart's 'Spring' song, *Sehnsucht nach dem*

Frühling, is simply a ditty of folkistic simplicity, a light-hearted melody, spring-like certainly – but in no sense probing; the melody repeated in the treble of the accompaniment, a simple Alberti figure in the bass. A comparative Schubert song on the longing for spring, say *Frühlingstraum* ('Dream of Spring', from *Winterreise*, D911) sets out on a remarkably similar 6/8 basis. But after ten bars of a fairly uncomplicated strain (although there has been a brief flirtation with the relative minor), Schubert starts to explore; the cock discordantly crows and the centre portion begins to dramatise the words and leads us to a slow frostbound section. The repeat indulges in several small subtleties by way of variation and the song which started in A major ends in A minor. This is not an altogether fair comparison if it suggests that Mozart never wrote anything but simple strophic songs. Schubert did too, for example *Heidenröslein* ('Hedge-rose'), but it is a fair illustration of the expansion of ideas that Schubert demonstrated on a similar theme.

As mentioned earlier, Schubert's ideas on songwriting were by no means all his own. Composers like Johann Rudolf Zumsteeg (1760–1802), however little their reputations mean today, had well trodden some of the paths that he was to follow. But then so had gifted composers for two hundred years or so. It was, however, the fresh insight into word-setting, coupled with an irrepressible melodic impulse, that made Schubert's songs seem so much less intellectual and self-conscious than much that was written before them and since. It was, most of all, their spontaneity. The wonder of many Schubert songs is not that lyricism contrives to seem profound, but that profundity manages to remain so lyrical. Where other *Lieder* writers often seem to lose touch with the beauty of the human voice, straining it into all kinds of contrived postures, Schubert's *Lieder* are always 'songs' in which the voice never loses its flow, pulse or grace. This may partly be due, as has been said on several occasions, to Schubert's own limitations both as a pianist and a singer, as well as his natural affinity with the popular song, so that he always wrote music that could be understood, mastered and made enjoyable by limited exponents. His songs do not need virtuoso singers and pianists to perform them. The most successful readings often come from the less showy artists who simply exhibit a clear understanding of their texts.

So, with the examples of such as Reichardt, Zelter and Zumsteeg to hand, Schubert set out, in a mood of explorative exhilaration, to set words to music so that both gained from the other's strengths. He was very much aware from an early stage that it was the combined forces that mattered. He got round to mentioning it in a letter, in 1825, when he reported on a concert with his friend Vogl: 'The way Vogl sings these things, and I accompany him – so that while the performance lasts we seem to be one – is a quite unheard-of novelty.' He set out in a remarkable way by clearly emulating one of Zumsteeg's long-winded cantatas for solo voice and in March 1811 produced some twenty-eight pages of manuscript which was a setting of Schücking's *Hagars Klage* ('*Hagar's Lament*', D5), first published in 1781 and set by Zumsteeg in 1797. Spaun firmly asserts that Schubert was merely setting out to modernise Zumsteeg's version, but obviously got carried away with his work and laid before his teacher Salieri a remakable piece which, with its dramatic accompaniments, could well have suggested to him a future writer of opera. Apart from a few minor harmonic quirks already showing, it demonstrates a remarkable understanding of what is suited to the voice and is still effective in performance. Similar pieces followed – *Des Mädchens Klage* ('*The Maiden's Lament*', D6); *Eine Leichenphantasie* ('*Corpse Fantasy*': D7) and *Der Vatermörder* (D10). The first of these has already found him using the words of Schiller. They all lead, with over-heavy dramatic steps, to the pages of his first opera *Der Spiegelritter*. Salieri strongly advised him to keep off the German poets and to work with the more melifluous Italian of such as Metastasio, with whom he often worked himself. In some pieces for various combinations of voices – such as *Quell'innocente figlio* (D17) – he follows this advice by way of exercises; and the manuscript bears corrections by Salieri. Similar exercises (D33–35) were dutifully attempted, but Schubert may well have felt that the Italian gloss was not for him. His next vocal trios move to Germanic fields. Vocal quartets and trios, usable in the school, dominated his output for some time, although his first version of Schiller's *Der Jüngling am Bache* ('*The young man by the brook*'; D30) begins to show signs of the *echt* Schubert. This is most strongly detected in a setting of words by Alexander Pope (translated by Herder) – 'The dying Christian to his Soul' – in German *Verklärung* (D59). Johann Gottfried Herder (1744–1803) was an important figure in German literature, an ardent collector and translator of folk-song and author of several important books on song, language and philosophy. It was the 'Death where is thy sting?' lines of Pope that became important to Schubert in Herder's German, providing the sort of unified text that was to create a unified song. In his friends Spaun and Holzapfel he found delightful fellow conspirators, all delighting in rummaging through the pages of German poetry in defiance of Salieri's recommended preference for the Italian, a language that, when required, provides a quickly nutritious soil for plants with shallow roots. Schubert and his friends were greatly stirred by the news of Theodor Körner's death in battle in 1813. Schubert had met him a few months before and had been much impressed on meeting such an attractively heroic figure. Yet the trumpetings of war were not really the material of Schubert's genius. Schiller's romantic sentimentality was perhaps less elevated, but it was nearer to the humanistic drama that Schubert was seeking. Following Körner's death, he decided to devote himself entirely to composition and he made a start in 1814 by devoting much of his selective effort of that year to songwriting. Notable amongst these were *Der Abend* ('*Evening*'; D108), which made a distinct move away from the heavy balladry of his early years, and *Lied der Liebe* ('*Song of Love*'; D109) both of which clearly lead toward the first true vocal masterpiece *Gretchen am Spinnrade* ('Margaret at the spinning-wheel'; D118), which Fischer-Dieskau has described as 'the birth of the essential, the great Schubert *Lied*'. To some extent it was the selection of texts that promoted success. This was Schubert's first association with the words of Goethe and there is no doubt that he found in them the true strength and flow that he needed. The song appeared out of the blue, not quite like anything that singers had been asked to sing before. The accompaniment is no longer just bass support; it has become the spinning wheel itself. It portrays the monotony of the task; it falters when the desparing Gretchen falters; it is a uniform accompaniment, yet full of infinite subtle variation. In draining the poem's subject, Schubert also drains the singer and pianist. The voice has to achieve three climaxes in its exhaustion. The pianist has to keep up a physical background that, like many Schubert accompaniments, tends to induce paralysis of the arm. The other important association of 1814 came when Johann Mayrhofer (1787–1836) was introduced to the Schubert circle by Spaun. Mayrhofer had once intended to be a priest, later studied law and finally found himself in the civil service. All these respectable leanings merely disguised a would-be poet of great talent, who was to supply Schubert with many texts, next in number only to Goethe. He had much in common with Schubert. He had a gruff, serious nature, a head full of deep thoughts, rarely laughed or indulged in frivolity, and did not have much time for women. He became the composer's closest friend and later they were to share rooms for two years. Schubert set his texts often as a result of the friendship rather than on the strength of their ultimate merits, yet no doubt he found a fascination in their constant changes of direction and mood in midstream. He first knew of Mayrhofer when he set *Am See* ('By the lake'; D124) just before they became acquainted.

From tentative and searching beginnings Schubert really got into his stride as a songwriter in the year 1815. It was a year that saw the production of no less than 145 songs, including such contrasting items as *Heidenröslein* in August and *Erlkönig* in the late autumn. The folky spontaneity of many of the songs is a reflection of the circumstances of their production. They were mainly intended for the enjoyment of a close circle of friends, literary rather than musical, to be sung and heard at evenings which generally began with poetry readings and ended with a visit to some favourite drinking haunt, lasting until the early hours of the morning. Schubert would bring settings of poems by his friends, often poems of no great merit yet which he has used as a basic ingredient for compositions of great ingenuity and depth. Perhaps he even enjoyed the freedom that an inconsequential lyric gave him. But as well as enjoying hearing their own works, the friends would also read and discuss the works of the better-known and established poets; amongst them Goethe, the great name of German literature.

Schubert's friends had no doubt, even at this time, that his works ought to be published and widely appreciated. Between them they planned several volumes with the songs arranged in groups according to the poets: a very forward-looking conception that was not taken up by wider outside interests until half a decade after Schubert's death. The idea came to nothing, but one group, those set to Goethe's poems, seemed to be a possible source of good publicity, particularly if Goethe himself could be persuaded to recognise their merits. So, in April 1816, Josef Spaun took it upon himself to write to the great man in humble and fawning tones, enclosing sixteen songs which Schubert had painstakingly copied in a neat legible hand and had bound together. It included *Heidenröslein*, *Gretchem am Spinnrade*, *Rastlose Liebe* ('Restless love') and ended with *Erlkönig*. They were the works, said Spaun in his letter, 'of a musician aged nineteen, Franz Schubert by name, whom nature had endowed from childhood with the most pronounced leanings toward the art of music, gifts brought to maturity with the help of the great Salieri'. Spaun somewhat exaggerated the general acclamation that these songs had already aroused and spoke grandly of their coming publication in volumes based on various poets, the first two by Goethe, followed by volumes devoted to Schiller, Klopstock and others. Permission to dedicate the first volumes to Goethe was submissively requested, the writer feeling certain that the obvious merits of the songs would be appreciated by Goethe who had only to reply in 'two words'. But even this modest request met with no response. Not even one word was heard from Goethe, although the volume was carefully returned. Goethe was known for his reticence in these matters, and was no doubt inundated with such missives and endless musical settings. His diaries and letters never even intimated the composer's existence throughout his lifetime. Schubert, however, continued to express his admiration of Goethe's genius; and Schubert's friends remained undiminished in their high regard of his.

1817 saw the production of some sixty songs, including *Der Tod und das Mädchen* ('Death and the Maiden'; D531), *Ganymed* (D544), *An die Musik* ('To music'; D547) and *Die Forelle* ('The Trout'; D550). It was also the significant year in which Schubert and the well-known singer Johann Michael Vogl first met. Vogl did not offer immediate enthusiasm but made a few vaguely encouraging noises. He performed some of the songs with splendid style, altering whatever he felt like altering, and was obviously secretly impressed. Schubert, thus encouraged, sent a copy of *Erlkönig* to Breitkopf & Härtel in Leipzig, offering it for publication. The publishers rejected it with scarcely a thought (although they published Schubert's *Complete Works* toward the end of the century, they accepted nothing in his lifetime) and returned it in error to a double-bass playing composer in the service of the Saxon Court in Dresden who also happened to be named Franz Schubert. He wrote to the publishers and indignantly refuted any connection with 'that sort of trash' but said that he intended to keep the manuscript so that he could find out 'the fellow who has thus misused my name'. Eventually Schubert got his song back. Meanwhile he was humbly pleased by any kind remarks that came his way and wrote to Josef Hüttenbrenner in 1818, thanking him for his appreciation and enclosing a copy of *Die Forelle*. Around this time he was able to bask in some of his earliest favourable press comments, discerningly written by Franz von Schlechta in the *Theaterzeitung*, on a performance of one of his Overtures 'in the Italian style' which the critic described as 'wondrously lovely'.

He had to wait until 1819 for the first of his songs to be sung in public. Again the *Theaterzeitung* was lavish in its appreciation of *Schäfers Klagelied* ('Shepherd's lament') by Goethe, with music by Herr Franz Schubert, sung by Herr Jäger, opera singer at the Theater an der Wien. A beautiful composition, sung most feelingly in Herr Jäger's enchanting voice'. Other critics found the work variously 'amusing', 'sensitive' and 'enjoyable'. How Jäger came across the yet unpublished piece is not clear. The occasion was a charity concert which was rather poorly attended. Contrary to the acceptance of most of Schubert's writings, the reception for *Erlkönig*, a highly dramatic piece in an accepted mould, was enjoyably and justly favourable, and no doubt heartened its composer considerably.

By 1820 he was also enjoying some modest praise for his operetta *Die Zwillingsbrüder*, which some assumed to be his first stage work. He had, in fact, already written six without success. 1821, the year in which he wrote the two *Suleika* songs (D717 and 720) and the shapely *Sei mir gegrüsst* ('I send you greetings'; D741), he received a sparkling testimonial from Count Moritz Dietrichstein, Court Music Chamberlain, who spoke of his 'innate genius' and promise; and his *Erlkönig* was sung at a Gesellschaft der Musickfreunde concert in January by Herr von Gymnich, a founder-member of 1812, who introduced Schubert glowingly to the assembled intellectuals. It was sung again the following month, together with *Sehnsucht* ('Longing'), and then in March by Michael Vogl, accompanied by Anselm Hüttenbrenner, at a Grand Concert at the Kärntnerthor Theater. It was hailed as 'showing much imagination'. The praise was somewhat clouded by the same critic's poor opinion of the part-song 'Song of the Spirits Over the Water'. Praise for *Erlkönig* seemed universal ('the glorious *Erlkönig* by our so greatly promising Schubert'), and it was a fitting beginning to his career as a published composer when it became his first work to be printed (in April 1821) with a permitted dedication to His Excellency, Count Moritz von Dietrichstein. His printed Op. 2 was the earlier masterpiece *Gretchen am Spinnrade*; and the publication of his songs became a regular occurrence, attended by fairly generous praise which to some extent countermands the view of Schubert as a totally neglected composer. Certainly, he got a fair share of his due as a songwriter, even if he was less than generously dealt with in other spheres. In March 1822, the *Wiener Zeitschrift für Kunst* published an article 'A Glance at Schubert's Songs' (Opp. 1–7) by Friedrich von Hentl (who was well acquainted with him), which muddles up a few of the titles but otherwise shows a fair discernment of their qualities, with *Erlkönig* predictably hailed as Schubert's greatest work. In summary he found that they revealed 'the marks of genius and of a thinking artist'.

What may well have surprised many of the contemporary critics, even though Schubert would have appeared more of a modernist to them than he does to us, was the constant lyricism and melodic flow that even today lifts Schubert far above the run of more academic *Lieder* writers in the estimation of both the general and the more critical public. The natural desire to delight never submerged the thinking side of his art. We suspect that, in fact, his art was mainly intuitive, for the technicalities of music are almost never discussed in his letters or diaries. An appraisal of the countless superbly wrought, often perfectly conceived, often insistently unforgettable songs of Schubert is beyond the scope of this book. They have been adequately dealt with in such excellent studies as Richard Capell's *Schubert's Songs* and Dietrich Fischer-Dieskau's *Schubert: a Biographical Study of His Songs*, and various valuable chapters elsewhere. Schubert was not only a *Lieder* writer (with whatever highbrow meaning that implies) but also a songwriter in the modern sense, as we would apply it to some inspired exception to the Tin Pan Alley production line standards, such as Jerome Kern. Each crafted article was intended to please, a concept sometimes seen as of gravely dubious merit in today's over-serious music-making.

Perhaps the most significantly successful section of songwriting that Schubert produced was in the song-cycle *Die schöne Müllerin* ('The fair maid of the mill'; D795), a form repeated with equal success but darker significance in *Winterreise*, for both of which the poet was Wilhelm Müller. In Schubert's isolated songs we can discern plenty of directed craft producing a significant as well as a pleasing result. In *Die schöne Müllerin* we can enjoy a sustained effort on the same level, a succession of songs that have a theme and tell a story, almost on operatic lines. And what an opera Schubert could have written had he put such music into it as this! Müller was a North German poet, a freedom-fighter in the Napoleonic wars, who shared Schubert's implied belief that the arts were for the people. If this occasionally led him to the verges of banality, the sincerity and simplicity of his poems greatly appealed to Schubert and inspired him to a similar directness of expression. Having discovered Müller's volume, he wrote part of the cycle in hot haste, left it for a while as he had to attend to *Fierrabras* and spend an embarrassing period in hospital, and then returned to it at the end of 1823. The final cycle was published in March 1824 as Op. 25, dedicated to the tenor Baron Carl von Schönstein, another friend who often sang and publicised his music. The press and others were fairly quiet about this latest effort, perhaps overwhelmed by twenty songs in one go.

The naive tenderness and directness of Müller's *Die schöne Müllerin* led Schubert to produce works of uncomplicated genius. Deeper poetry, such as Goethe's, led him to deeper music; Müller inspired his most graceful and lyrical muse. Almost half are simply strophic in form; the rest in a continuous flowing form that *Gretchen* had inaugurated, the flowing of the brook continually implied in many moods. It was a true cycle achieved with few predecessors to guide him. Some of the songs are too short to be effective on their own, almost too folky and popular in aspect. Together they add up to a telling whole. Leaving out the original Prologue and Epilogue from Müller's sequence and three songs given to the Miller, Schubert set twenty items that range from the decorated folksong nature of *Das Wandern* ('Wandering') and *Wohin?* ('Whither?', a song based on *Daphne am Bach* written in 1816) to the isolated *Der Neugierige* ('The Eager Questioner') which stands aside for a moment, to the final depth and sadness of *Der Müller und der Bach* ('The Miller and the Brook') and *Wiegenlied* ('Lullaby'). Such a song-cycle, so full of meaning and shadow, so open to interpretation, is liable to tempt singers to many dramatic excesses. It is the nature of Schubert's songs, never more than here, that they respond well to an eminently musical and simplistic approach.

The comparatively carefree, if ever melancholy, Schubert was a very different person from the infinitely sadder, even depressingly wiser, man of 1827 who wrote *Winterreise* (D911; 'Winter Journey'). It kept him away from the warm friendship of the Schubertiads; and when Spaun asked him the cause of his absence, he replied, 'you will soon hear and understand'. He promised to bring his latest works to Schober's a while later and asked his friends to come to hear 'a cycle of frightening songs'. Which he did, and they were much taken aback and perturbed by the sombre sadness that they heard. Schober told him that he only liked *Der Lindenbaum* ('The Linden Tree'), but Schubert declared that these were the songs that he most liked himself and that others would come to think the same.

In *Der Leiermann* ('The Organ-grinder') he mournfully saw his own fate in that of the organ-grinder to whom nobody wanted to listen. Much of the credit for these great moments in song must go to Müller, who rarely gets his full due. But again it was a case of Schubert finding his ideal text and then wringing the utmost musical meaning from it; more so because it fitted the despair of his last years so painfully well. The technical differences between this cycle and *Die schöne Müllerin* are slight but there is a wealth of difference in the feel and depth of the two cycles. Wilhelm Müller died as Schubert was setting his words. A year later Schubert was in his final illness, correcting the proofs of *Winterreise* in lucid moments. It is such intimate music that Fischer-Dieskau was moved to ask the question: 'Should one perform *Die Winterreise* in public at all?' The answer was, of course, yes – but only if the full chilling morbidity of the work is put over without restraint and the audience is prepared to accept the experience.

The discerning *Theaterzeitung* critical pages, on the publication of the first part of the cycle, saw a work that 'none can sing or hear without being deeply moved . . . and we are borne through the immeasurable depths of the human heart into worlds beyond'. So, again we should be careful not to overstate the impression that there was no one capable of appreciating Schubert in his time. Even so, there was no great rush to publish his songs in substantial collections. It was 1834 before Charles Simon Richault in Paris came out with his *40 Mélodies de Fr. Schubert*, which contained such strange-sounding items as '*Sois toujours mes seuls amours*' (which turns out to be *Sei mir gegrüsst*). It also contained, by what quirk of fate or judgment is not known, a song called *Adieu* which became a tremendously popular 'Schubert' item, frequently transposed for piano, and still to be found in the 1896 Boosey edition of *Sixty Songs* edited by J.A. Kappey and many later collections. It was, in fact, a song by August Heinrich von Weyrauch, and had already been published by its composer under the title of *Nach Osten* in 1824.

If things took their place with dramatic rightness in proper cinematic terms, Schubert would have rounded off his working life with something of profound tragic significance. But what do we find at the end of the Deutsch catalogue but a mainly cheerful piece in the Rossini vein, *Der Hirt auf dem Felsen* ('The Shepherd on the Rocks'; D965) with a lightly melodic accompanying part for piano and clarinet (or cello). Some people prefer to think that the melancholy *Taubenpost* ('Pigeon Post') was Schubert's vocal farewell; but some may prefer the quirkishnss of *Der Hirt* which presumably was composed, with no thoughts of mortality, for the virtuosic purposes of Anna Milder-Hauptmann in Berlin. She had asked for the work to be written; but she did not receive her copy until September 1829 when Ferdinand Schubert forwarded a copy by way of Michael Vogl.

A final comment on Schubert the songwriter might aptly be on the infinite serviceability of his music. There have been few composers who have provided a corpus of songs that can be so liberally transposed for every voice from lowest bass to highest soprano without undue damage to their effect. Is it perhaps the essential musicality of them that allows this? They also, for the same reasons, transpose well into piano music or as solos for cello or violin – or, in fact, almost anything you care to mention. Change their accent slightly and, as we know, they could slip well into the world of the popular theatre. They are held in the highest possible esteem by nearly everyone.

V Schubert's position as a composer

An evaluation of Schubert's position and rating in the years immediately after his death has to be made on the basis of many conflicting opinions and assessments. The first point in the reckoning is always that he was greatly overshadowed by Beethoven who enjoyed the privilege of being justly assessed as a great genius in his own lifetime. But he was also greatly overshadowed by a number of lesser writers who had achieved wide publication in their lifetime, particularly those who were also highly acclaimed executive musicians like Hummel, Moscheles and Paganini. Even many names that are virtually meaningless today like Romberg (not Sigmund but Andreas) and Ries had their works extensively published and played. An often quoted fact is that the British musicologist Edward Holmes went to Vienna in 1828 to write a piece about the musical life there and did so without a single mention of Schubert's name. This has always seemed incredible in connection with a composer who, the following year, was going to be buried next to Beethoven; but it was likely that Holmes got into a different set of establishment musicians and was just not there when Schubert was being performed. Nevertheless this trend, outside Vienna, certainly continued for some time. A popular London compilation *The Musical Library*, published by Charles Knight & Co. in 1837, has no Schubert in its 'instrumental' volumes – though, again, such names as Hummel, Kalkbrenner, Kuhlau, Moscheles, Ries and Romberg are all well represented.

Even within Vienna there was a remarkable lack of attention to the passing of the city's greatest native musical genius. The gentleman who reported on Viennese music for the London magazine *Harmonicon* had much to say about Louis Spöhr that month (reports of whose death had previously been exaggerated) but had heard nothing of Schubert's passing. Six months later the news had got through to him. He reported that amongst Schubert's belongings were to be found twelve grand operas, five operettas, eight masses, ten symphonies, etc., etc. – but went on to discuss at greater length the Requiem that Anselm Hüttenbrenner wrote for the funeral. None of Schubert's music, published or hidden, was played. Ferdinand Schubert did his best to sort out the vast pile of manuscripts that his brother had left behind and tried to get some of it printed. He was particularly keen that the symphonies should be published, but met with no success in this venture. The first sale of Schubert's belongings included the songs (sold to Tobias Haslinger for 500 florins) written to poems by Rellstab and Heine which were to be issued as *Schwanengesang*. Three Grand Sonatas and Schubert's final song, *Der Hirt auf dem Felsen*, which was published in 1830, were also sold.

Had Schubert died with the public memory of nine great symphonies left behind, of course things might have been different– or a number of majestic concertos that he had performed – or even a few known operas! But his main contribution to music, to general knowledge, was chamber and piano music and the audience for that sort of thing is limited. Otherwise he was known as a songwriter and that too has a limited appeal; although many of his works had become common property often without acknowledgment to him. A touching and discerning obituary notice in the Philharmonic Society bulletin in February 1829, written by his friend Sonnleithner, mentions three symphonies and details twelve operas, but openly says that much of his music was still unknown to the public.

The various notices of 1829, 1830 and immediately ensuing years are fairly and enthusiastically written, with due regard to the limits of their writers' total knowledge of Schubert's achievement. But again most of them came from friends trying to promote his cause as best they could. The first sizeable article was written by Josef von Spaun (and revised by Anton Ottenwalt) in the spring of 1829. It certainly contained enough substance and justification for Schubert's survival. Publishers soon began to make amends for their previous neglect; or, more likely, simply cast an opportunist eye on a probable source of income. The publisher Josef Czerny claimed to have acquired the major part of his works, including a Grand Quintet for Piano and Strings (the 'Trout' Quintet) which was rightly claimed to be a masterpiece. But Czerny had no knowledge of the true extent of Schubert's writing. Diabelli publicised their more justifiable claims to being Schubert's publisher (even if it was mainly at someone else's expense). By 1835 there were various references to Schubert as a 'genius', but Ferdinand was still struggling to get the major works published. He wrote his own account of the composer's life and works for the Leipzig *Neue Zeitschrift für Musik* in April/May 1839.

It took someone with real insight into Schubert's art and genius, with some power of communication, to set things rolling in a wave of posthumous appreciation. One such person was the young composer and critic Robert Schumann who was only eighteen or so when Schubert died. It was some years before he had much power or influence, but eventually he wrote discerningly and emotively about Schubert and paid tribute to him in his own compositions. For years he bought everything of Schubert's that he could find and then, on New Year's Day 1839, arranged to pay a visit to Ferdinand Schubert's house to try to find out a little more about the composer. He was delighted and astonished to find the house still full of unpublished works. One of these was the 'Great' C major Symphony, which he persuaded Breitkopf & Härtel to publish. It had its first public performance under Mendelssohn in 1839. Not that it immediately became a popular work, for it proved too taxing for the string players in most orchestras of the day.

Schubert appreciation tended to stand at the ebb and it was not until the decades of 1850–60 that a real appreciation of his true stature began. The first full-length biography by Heinrich

Kreissle von Hellborn appeared in Vienna in 1865. Even by then it was getting too late to obtain information from people who had known Schubert and worked with him. Already memories were beginning to take on the strange colours that time lends. 1865 was, too, the year that Herbeck brought the 'Unfinished' Symphony to light. The London edition of Kreissle's biography in 1869 was made even more significant by an appendix contributed by the distinguished London musicologist, George Grove, who had begun to appreciate Schubert around 1846–7, having come across a few of his songs at that time. He heard the C major Symphony played under August Manns at the Crystal Palace in April 1856. It was its first performance and Manns' own first acquaintance with the work, which he heard of through the promotional efforts of Schumann and Mendelssohn. A story he tells gives an insight into tastes of the time: 'I have reason to believe,' he wrote in a letter published some forty years later, 'that my performance of the C major Symphony in 1856 was the first in England, although I remember hearing one of the members of my then very small band speak of a rehearsal of it under the late Dr Wylde, when, at the close of the first movement, the principal horn called out to one of the first violins: "Tom, have you been able to discover a tune yet?" "I have *not*," was Tom's reply.' Grove's interest was thoroughly roused. He still believed that this was the only symphony that Schubert had written. He reports that the feeble performance by the small orchestra did little to arouse much enthusiasm except in his own mind. Later he heard the Overture to *Rosamunde*, another favourite of Manns', and was anxious to know what else was in this score. The publication of Kreissle's biography excited him greatly and the catalogue, which listed more of the *Rosamunde* music, he found particularly interesting. He wrote to Spina in Vienna, who had taken over the Diabelli catalogue, and Spina sent him newly published versions of the two entr'actes, which were first played in London in November 1866, together with the Romance, sung by Mademoiselle Enequist. The Overtures to *Alfonso und Estrella* and *Fierrabras*, and the Overture in the Italian Style in C, followed and were performed in 1867. The 'Unfinished' Symphony had been published in 1867 and was first played under Manns on 6 April 1867. This was the final stimulation. Enlisting the help and companionship of another Schubert enthusiast, Arthur Sullivan, Grove departed for Vienna to see Spina and get permission to browse around his offices. They found the scores of the First, Second, Third, Fourth and Sixth Symphonies, which Ferdinand had earlier tried to get Diabelli to publish, and eagerly set about copying them. This task done, they searched further and found the original manuscripts of several operas. But there was still the principal object missing. On the Thursday before the weekend they were due to depart, they had one more diligent look. Grove delved into the back of a deep and dusty cupboard and there he found, still bound up after their last performance, and placed in a box, the orchestral parts of the whole of the *Rosamunde* music. They managed to make a copy of all the parts before they left Vienna. Grove also reports on the treasures they left behind – *Lazarus*, masses, chamber music and so much beside. At last the treasure vaults of Schubert's music had been opened and the world was about to be aware of its true extent. On his return Grove wrote, at the end of his contributed appendix to the English edition of Kreissle:

> As for Schubert, his place in the world is certain. Whether his Symphonies and Operas are published and performed now, or twenty years later, is not of much importance to his fame. He can afford to wait. They will assuredly be done some day or other, and then the world will find out what it has lost by waiting so long, and wonder that it did not recognise its jewel sooner. Certainly what poor Schubert said was right, that the music that was the fruit of his distress had given the world most pleasure; and the world seems to have known it, for it kept him in his poverty and harassment and disappointment, till he died of it. Good God! it makes one's blood boil to think of so fine and rare a genius, one of the ten or twelve topmost

men in the world, in want of even the common necessities of life.

In 1879 Grove began to publish the first edition of his famous *Dictionary of Music and Musicians* and his fine piece on Schubert became the standard reference to the composer for many years. In Vienna Mandyczewski was busy preparing the 'complete' edition of Schubert's works, which were to be published between 1884 and 1897. The dates of the world's discovery of, for example, the Symphonies, are deplorable but fascinating. After their first amateur performances, their first complete public performances came as follows: the First in 1881 in London; the Second in 1877 in London; the Third in 1881 in London; the Fourth in 1849 in Leipzig; the Fifth in 1873 in London; the Sixth in 1828 in Vienna; the Seventh (completed sketch) in 1883 in London; the Eighth in 1865 in Vienna; the Ninth in 1839 in Leipzig. London, via Grove and Manns, takes a great deal of the credit, in these instances, for the discovery of Schubert.

Appreciation of Schubert, from the days of Grove, became an accepted thing and he took his place alongside the other great composers in the histories and textbooks. As a footnote, it is incredible to find Richard Capell writing to the *Daily Telegraph* as late as 1950 to complain that Schubert's last symphony was being played at the Albert Hall as his seventh. Long after you could still buy the Eulenberg miniature score so numbered. He went on to list them in what he then assumed to be their proper order; going on to point out that the haphazard way that Schubert's works appear in all the popular editions is nothing less than a scandal. 'The quartets numbered by Eulenberg as 1–9 are, as a matter of fact, Nos. 13, 7, 11, 15, 9, 14, 10, 8 and 12: and similarly the piano sonatas numbered 1–10 in Augener's edition are Nos. 16, 17, 13, 6, 14, 8, 9, 19, 20 and 21.' The Novello edition of eleven sonatas in two volumes, edited by Köhler and Ruthardt, almost followed the same order, which was, of course, mainly a result of adherence to the original published opus numbers.

Reliance on Nottebohm's *Thematic Catalogue* of 1874 (which

listed 900 works) and on the Breitkopf & Härtel edition, plus the original opus numbers, left Schubert's output in confusion until 1950 when Otto Erich Deutsch first published his invaluable and generally accurate *Thematic Catalogue*. It was a great step forward for musical mankind.

So how should we rate Schubert in the hierarchy of music? Many would simply declare that he must be placed amongst the world's greatest; a few, afflicted with the distorted vision that arises from a love affair, have even called him the greatest of all. Personally I would say, without a tremor of doubt, that Schubert is the composer I most love and cherish; though he is closely jostled for that position by Mozart – the composer I most admire. Some of Schubert's music has not been surpassed by anyone. But there is really no harm in putting his most sublime achievements into the perspective of his curiously erratic achievement, incomplete and inconsistent if we put it beside the achievement of Mozart.

His orchestral output was not negligible but it shrinks into insignificance beside the consistently elevated output of other major composers. However delightedly and often we play his pianistic miniatures and isolated pieces, it is still arguable that he did not manage to produce an impressive sequence of sonatas. In itself erratic, his chamber music can probably be put alongside anyone's without suffering from the comparison. The musical world remains bemused by his operas. These may never grace the stage but they will certainly be rediscovered as music and song. His exact contemporary Donizetti turned out stageable operas with remarkable ease and turned plots as unlikely as any that Schubert tackled into satisfactory drama. Yet he never came anywhere near matching Schubert's potential as a composer. In the end, of course, we rest our defence on the fact that has been stated a thousand times: that Schubert was the greatest songwriter of all. No one else holds a candle to him here, either in quantity or quality. And, in popular terms, he achieved as many hit tunes to remember as a Berlin or a Rodgers.

So one tries, as we have already done, to reason why and to ask a few wherefores. The first consideration was simply the nature of the man. That he often achieved the greatest of greatness, the acme of genius, is beyond question; but there is little visible evidence that he was a great man in the ordinary human sense. He was a shy, obstinate, self-sufficient, undisciplined and somewhat comical character. He frequently passed Beethoven in the street but never dared speak to him. Would his work have been better had he been a close acquaintance of Beethoven and an avowed disciple, rather than indulging in friendship with a lot of very minor composers? We may doubt it. His music would certainly have been different but probably a lot less interesting, and it would have included a lot more second-rate Beethoven. His friendships were drawn substantially from literary, artistic and political circles. He liked warm companionship and found it much enhanced by alcoholic consumption. Was there perhaps even a touch of indolence about him, though he was one of the most prolific of all composers, who wrote over a thousand works in twenty or so years? But even the facts of his output have been exaggerated. If you do nothing but write music there is no reason why, given the faculty, you should not write a great deal. A large percentage of these thousand works were short songs. With a remarkable facility he would often write several in a day; some of them perhaps took an hour to put down. 1815 (the year he really set out to be a composer) and 1816 were remarkable years, in both of which he wrote some 200 works (but then there are 365 days in a year); thereafter forty (or less) works per annum was a steady average. Not all that prolific.

It is the natural course of musical appreciation applied to individuals after their demise, and the lack of recognition that often goes with being alive, that posterity soon begins to add legend to the life and glory to the achievement. Nowadays earnest writings appear that attempt to persuade us that Schubert was a great writer of piano sonatas. I am afraid that I cannot see that they have changed much since they were considered as merely interesting and individual. No doubt somewhere a book is simmering that will finally prove him to be a great but neglected writer of opera. These works will deserve and will get adequate productions and recordings; with a little rewriting of the librettos not going amiss. We have rescued Schubert's other music from the great oblivion of his lifetime and the reluctant acceptance of the nineteenth century. We have put him on his proper pedestal and we acknowledge the divine spark; but we should not go overboard in trying to prove anything to the detriment of others striving for promotion to a higher division.

As for the attempt to make his life, in common with all other lives, seem like a god-like dream of hourly inspiration – the writing of great music does not turn a man into a god. There have been horrified recoils at some views taken of Schubert's life; in films and musicals, and so on. What Berté did in *Das Dreimädelhaus* ('The House of Three Maidens'; later adapted by Clutsam as *Lilac Time*) has really aroused the ire of the cloistered scholars. The 'unpleasant handiwork of Berté' who 'popularised Schubert in so painful a manner' were words used with great indignation in the *Music Review* of the 1940s. What exactly was unpleasant and painful, and what was wrong in popularising Schubert? What is ever wrong with popularising a composer? It makes him no less worthy or satisfying to his well-mannered devotees. Maybe *Lilac Time* went a little too far in making him the romantic, dallying, wine-bibing Richard Tauber type; but, what is far more important, it made discerning use of some of his minor yet, in its way, important music – naturally, of a melodic nature – finding all kinds of half-hidden gems in songs, small piano pieces and stage music that has made at least some of his music common property. However, it should never be allowed to hide the fact that one side of him was a serious, dedicated and profound composer.

The best biography is quite simply the sort produced by Deutsch – 'documentary'. The facts, the contemporary writings and opinions, the composer's own words (however few) are put before us. We draw our own conclusions with the aid of the music Schubert produced. Out of this, we may find Schubert a rather odd, even comical, little man, inadequate in coping with daily problems, frequently in hiding like a shellfish. From those hidden moments, which he shared with nobody, came lots of manuscript paper and many moments of divine magic.

What Schubert would have achieved had he not died at such an early (and, it would seem to modern science, unnecessary) age, will always be fruitless speculation. Certainly, one feels that he might well have pursued others in writing several great symphonies. Chamber music of even greater richness must have come. He would surely have resolved that operatic problem – one way or another. He might well have absorbed better what Weber and other romantics were doing, and headed towards the land of Wagner. Even more likely, I feel, he might have employed his undoubted talent for popular melody and found himself in the world of operetta, actually writing a *Lilac Time*. A *Fledermaus* would not have been beyond him had he met the right professional librettist. A little historical perspective helps here. It is not a remote world we are encountering when we read, in books about the Viennese waltz and the Strauss dynasty, that the Vienna Congress was the beginning of an era of great popular music-making. By the time Schubert died in 1828, Joseph Lanner (1801–43) was more than halfway through his successful career and the elder Johann Strauss (1804–49) likewise. It was only by a cat's whisker that Schubert was not drawn into this area. From this aspect his thirty-six *Original Tänze* (*genannt 'Erste Walzer'*) comprise one of the most remarkable collections of melodic snippets that we can find in musical history. The whole essence of Schubert is there: his questing harmonies and modulations; a melodic treasure based on the *Ländler* tradition. It was a spring that he could so easily have tapped, rather than leave it to the well-rewarded Berté and Clutsam a hundred years later.

Perhaps a little in defence of *Das Dreimädelhaus* (1916) should be appended here. With its offshoots it led many uncommitted souls to Schubert, and these operettas still have a great amateur following. The story was essentially a concocted one, with Schubert falling for one of three sisters (loosely based on the four

Fröhlich sisters who lived in the Spiegelgasse, near Graben), but being too shy, asks his friend (elevated to Baron) Schober to do the wooing. He does but Schober falls in love with her himself, leaving Schubert to music and dreams. Schwind and Kupelwieser also appear in the story. Maurice J.E. Brown has spoken, like others, of Heinrich Berté 'butchering' the purity and delicacy of the waltzes, and making pianists who might have played them steer clear of them because of their popularity. This not only seems a pure piece of musical snobbery, for familiarity does not make most people, apart from a few highbrows who cannot abide a melody anyway, like music any less. It is also less than fair to Heinrich Berté. His score, to some extent, avoided using all music that was blatantly familiar. He searched well and sensitively into the lesser-known piano pieces and the result really does pass as a very good operetta. His turning of the little gem of a waltz hidden in D783 into a song is a stroke of genius, effectively done and in excellent taste. Berté and his librettists are helped, of course, by their text being in German, thus fitting the music naturally. It is interesting, in this respect, to compare it with the French version which was called *Chanson d'Amour* or *La Maison de trois jeunes filles* (1922) with lyrics by Hugues Delorme and Léon Abric. It must be said that Clutsam's re-sorting of matters in *Lilac Time* (1922) is considerably less successful, viewed in a classical perspective (for it has been a great commercial success), partly because the English text, as is usual with translations, fits much less naturally, but also because he went farther than Berté in dragging in such familiar pieces, popular in their own right, as *Ständchen*, *Die Forelle*, *Heidenröslein* and the 'Unfinished' Symphony. These can sound a bit tasteless at times. A further adaptation for the American market was done by Sigmund Romberg as *Blossom Time* (also 1922) with 'Song of love' based on an 'Unfinished' theme becoming a popular hit. In 1934 there was a British film, starring Tauber, which had a somewhat different plot and music differently selected, also called *Blossom Time*; and this, in turn, was adapted for the stage under the same title by the industrious Clutsam.

All these may have changed the Schubert image to some, but they certainly made his music widely known and liked; and *Das Dreimädelhaus*, at least, should be given some credit for its ingenuity and reasonable taste. Schubert, with his tunefulness and his facility, might well have been one of the greatest popular composers of all time. The 'serious' musical world has long had a deplorable tendency to underrate anything that moves toward humour and lightness, regardless of the masterpieces that have been written in such a vein. Very often it is purely complexity, and even long-windedness, that gets praised because it seems more profound; whereas true inspiration has a tendency to look obvious once it has been discovered.

To recognise faults and failings is not to under-value merits and successes. It underlines them, rather, and throws them into prominence. History really played a strange trick with Schubert's music. It was largely suppressed in his own lifetime, partly through his personal shortcomings, partly through the usual obstacles that artistic commerce puts in the path of those upon whom it subsequently thrives. Partly, also, and perhaps most importantly, it was the music itself that was an obstacle. We come with surprise every now and then across what now seem strange outbursts against the difficulty, obtuseness and strangeness of Schubert's music. He certainly did things harmonically that must have sounded extremely odd to most ears (as did much of Beethoven's music, but which he had the power and virtuosity to promote); but, even more important, it was a new imaginative approach; what we can now perceive as the stirrings of romanticism. The later appreciation of Schubert's music came when it was being heard alongside music that had also reached the same historical and generative stage, when it no longer sounded odd. A lot of the contemporary impact is lost on us today. Putting it back into the perspective that time offers: many of us, in fact, find Schubert one of the vital keys to at least one of the many doors that musical history has to unlock. A very vital one, in fact; nothing less than the step from the 'classical' to the 'romantic' era – for what those loose terms are worth. There was an interesting article called 'The Classical Nature of Schubert's *Lieder*' by Walter Gray, which followed the premise that Schubert was the last great 'classicist' rather than the first great 'romanticist', especially in his songs. It is an interesting and valid point. It simply tosses around the point that is both obvious and puzzling in Schubert's music: that his means were classical and his imagination romantic. The turning point had been reached long before Schubert. Bach's slow movements have a romantic nature very often, by which we mean that personality and human warmth have become an element added to the architectural structure of music. Mozart's music contains so much of this romantic feeling, fascinatingly hidden in the elegant formality of his surface writing. Beethoven was different from the rest; he was so toweringly great that much of his music (particularly the symphonies and concertos) was simply an evocation of the spirit of Shakespeare or Michelangelo. But Schubert is one of those composers with whom we feel that the music is actually talking to us (particularly strongly in his best chamber music), expressing thoughts and feelings. Later it was a commonplace ability; but Schubert was one of the first to show how expressive music could be. In works like the beautifully proportioned Piano Trios or the underrated (because it is slight) 'Notturno', in the 'Death and the Maiden' quartet, in the 'Great' C major Symphony, we are best aware of the poise between classical objectivity and romantic subjectivity. Occasionally, in the C major Quintet, the B flat Piano Sonata and many of his best songs, we are in a world of musical thought unhampered by musical means. Surely it was this solitary search for such disembodied perfection that led to so many abandoned works, so many awkward attempts, so many mysterious moves. I am sure that the eternal and supreme interest in Schubert's music is that, as hardly anywhere else, we can feel and watch the process of a composer composing. Beethoven did something of the sort in his sketchbooks, but the final works have ironed out the problems with convincingly sweeping gestures. The whole of Schubert's music is something of a sketchbook; and some of the most fleeting and trivial sketches, with the luck attached to the artist who manages to get an exact likeness at the first attempt, often turn out to be finished masterpieces. But the whole concern of classical music-making, in writing it and, so it seems, even more so in writing about it, is in developing and building, extending things to controlled and effective lengths. The value of the miniature is consequently underrated. So often, Schubert (and many others) achieve such perfection in an opening phrase or theme that the subsequent labour of developing inevitably seems very much like gilding the lily. Some things are even better left unfinished.

Appendix

Throughout this book the invaluable Deutsch catalogue numbers to Schubert's works have been appended. They have largely superseded the old and totally unreliable opus numbers attached prior to Deutsch's researches and are used as a useful (if not totally decisive) aid to placing the works in their year of composition without the constant reiteration of such dates. As a rough guide the following table may be referred to:

1810	D1–2	1816	D331–510	1822	D734–767
1811	D3–10	1817	D511–598	1823	D768–797
1812	D11–35	1818	D599–632	1824	D798–822
1813	D36–91	1819	D633–678	1825	D823–862
1814	D92–124	1820	D679–708	1826	D863–895
1815	D125–330	1821	D709–733	1827	D896–936
				1828	D937–965

The only value of the opus numbers today is that they do give some indication of the order of publication of Schubert's works during his lifetime and in the immediately following years. Accounting for less than a fifth of the written works, they are an inadequate guide to his whole output and are frequently unhelpful. A number of works were also published in the composer's lifetime without being assigned opus numbers. Indicated dates of publication are as follows:

1821	Op. 1–9	1825	Op. 31–50
1822	Op. 10–14	1826	Op. 51–66 & Op. 69
1823	Op. 15–24 & Op. 30	1827	Op. 67–88 & Op. 62
1824	Op. 25–29	1828	Op. 89–108

Posthumously published works already given opus numbers by Schubert: Op. 98–105.

All subsequent numbers were applied at random by various publishers.

As noted in Deutsch's *Documentary Biography*, some 478 items were published in Schubert's lifetime, but this number includes many short songs and brief dances which were put together under one Deutsch number (sometimes as many as thirty-six) so that it does not represent the large percentage that it seems to. As Deutsch points out, the list included no symphonies or quintets, only one out of nineteen quartets, one of seven masses, no opera, twenty-two partsongs out of 135, and 187 songs out of a total of 600.

Select Bibliography

A selective list of books in English which supplement the present volume and have helped in its compilation:

Abraham, Gerald (editor). *Schubert: a Symposium.* London, Drummond, 1946.

BBC Guides: *Chamber Music* (J. A. Westrup); *Songs* (Maurice J. E. Brown); *Piano Sonatas* (Philip Radcliffe); *Symphonies* (Maurice J. E. Brown).

Brion, Marcel. *Daily Life in the Vienna of Mozart and Schubert.* London, Weidenfeld & Nicolson, 1961.

Brown, Maurice J. E. *Schubert: a Critical Biography.* London, Macmillan, 1958.

— *Essays on Schubert.* London, Macmillan, 1966.

Capell, Richard. *Schubert's Songs.* London, Duckworth, 1928; revised 1957; Pan Books, 1973.

Deutsch, Otto Erich (editor). *Franz Schubert's Letters and Other Writings.* London, Faber, 1928; New York, Books for Libraries, 1970.

Deutsch, Otto Erich. *Schubert: a Documentary Biography.* London, Dent, 1946; New York, Da Capo Press, 1977.

— *Schubert: Thematic Catalogue of all his Works.* London, Dent, 1951; New York, Kalmus, no date.

— *Schubert: Memoirs by his Friends.* London, Black, 1958.

Einstein, Alfred. *Schubert.* London, Cassell, 1952.

Fischer-Dieskau, Dietrich. *Schubert: A Biographical Study of his Songs.* London, Cassell, 1976.

Flower, Newman. *Franz Schubert: the Man and his Circle.* London, Cassell, 1928; revised 1949. (Useful bibliography.)

Gartenberg, Egon. *Vienna: its Musical Heritage.* Pennsylvania, State University Press, 1968.

Glock, William. 'Schubert' in *Lives of the Great Composers*, Vol. 2. (Ed. A. L. Bacharach.) London, 1935.

Hilmar, Ernst and Brusatti, Otto (editors). *Franz Schubert* (Vienna Catalogue) (German and English). Vienna, Universal Edition, 1978.

Hutchings, Arthur. *Schubert* (Master Musicians series). London, Dent, 1945; revised 1973.

Kreissle von Hellborn, Heinrich. *The Life of Franz Schubert* (2 Vols). London, Longmans Green, 1869.

Moore, Gerald. *The Schubert Song Cycles*. London, Hamish Hamilton, 1975.

Porter, Ernest G. *Schubert's Song Technique*. London, Dobson, 1961.

— *Schubert's Piano Works*. London, Dobson, 1980.

Reed, John. *Schubert: the Final Years*. London, Faber & Faber, 1972.

INDEX OF NAMES AND TITLES

WORKS BY SCHUBERT MENTIONED